SEVILLA Cathedral

Text

Francisco Gil Delgado

Photographs, diagrams and reproduction
entirely conceived and produced by
EDITORIAL ESCUDO DE ORO, S.A.

3rd Edition

I.S.B.N. 84-378-1678-5
Dep. Legal B. 34760-1998

Editorial Escudo de Oro, S.A.

View of the exterior of the Cathedral, south side.

Cathedral nave interior: vaults. ▷

SEVILLE CATHEDRAL

Interiors and exteriors

You are on the threshold of the largest cathedral in the world: in the glass cabinets next to the doors of San Miguel and Los Palos, are photocopies of the certificate from the Guinness Book of Records confirming this. The cathedral is 126.18 metres long by 82.60 metres wide. Its maximum height is 30.48 metres. This is not the longest cathedral in the world, however, but the one with the greatest surface area, taking into account the nave and four aisles and side chapels of the building.

This should come as no surprise. The Sevillian canons who decided that this cathedral should be built recommended that it should take this form. When Ferdinand III, the Holy, re-established Christianity in Seville after conquering the city from the Almohades on 23 November 1248, he did the same as he had done previously in Córdoba and in many other places: he converted the aljama mosque into a cathedral. This monarch, warlike and pious, also possessed a refined sense of respect for art. We can imagine what that mosque must have been like - much larger than that of Córdoba - from the space occupied by the Cathedral, from the huge dimensions of the adjoining courtyard of ablutions (now the Patio de los Naranjos) and from the magnificent minaret (the Giralda). In that mosque-cathedral, for a century and a half, were re-established the former principality of the Sevillian Church which, in the times of the Visigoths, under the

A part of the orange-tree patio with the roofs of the cathedral.

papacies of Saint Leander and Saint Isidoro, had reigned supreme throughout Hispania.

But the aljama was seriously damaged by an earthquake in 1356. Another, earthquake, in 1395, complicated things further. One day in the year 1401 (possibly 8 July), the canons had their awe-inspiring dream: "that the new church should be made such and so well that it should have no equal". The decision was the exclusive responsibility of the Chapter, as the place of archibishop had not been filled since the death, on 22 April, of Archbishop Gonzalo de Mena. Popular legend magnified the dream even further, as the story has been passed down from generation to generation that, as they left the Chapter session, the canons commented: "When it is complete, let posterity consider us all mad".

And here it stands before you, the unrealisable, gigantic dream, come true. To visit the different sections of Seville Cathedral is like visiting an artistic theme park. Less Romanesque (inevitably, as by the time Ferdinand III entered Seville the influence of the Gothic had already begun to spread) less Romanesque, but all periods of Christian art are represented here, as well as fine Visigoth remains, not forgetting the oppulence of Almohade art in the form of the Giralda and the Patio de los Naranjos.

Order of the visit. History and layout

We suggest that the visitor should accompany us, beginning exactly inside the main doorway, the Puerta de la Asunción, to which mystery the Cathedral is dedicated. In our visit, we will follow the stages of construction of the building, for even in this, Seville Cathedral is original. The first stone is believed to have been laid in 1403, blessed by Archbishop Alonso de Egea. But construction did not begin here, as was usual in Gothic churches, with the ambulatory, as this element was to be located at the head (east side) of the Cathedral where was the Capilla Real, with the tombs of Ferdinand III, Alphonse X, the Wise, and other royal personages. The king refused permission to demolish it, and the canons, therefore, so as not to lose impetus, decided to begin work at the foot of the church, the west side, which is where we now find ourselves. In the end, an ambulatory was never built in Seville Cathedral (amply replaced by the Capilla Real), so that the resulting groundplan was, in the words of Ceán Bermúdez, "quadrilonga" (rectangular) or *planta de salón*.

The interior of the Cathedral is a delight to the eyes: majestic nave and four aisles, supported by 36 rhomboid-shaped pillars embellished with beading in slender columns. They are thick, but the overall perspective makes them stylised, opening out like palm trees. Along with the half pillars adjoining the walls, they support 68 vaults made with stone from the quarries

Visigoth capitals. Chapel of La Granada.

Apse, the Giralda tower, symbol of Seville.

1498); Alonso Rodríguez (1496-1513); and Juan Gil de Hontañón (1513-1519). The design is Gothic (similar to Segovia Cathedal), of Germanic inspiration with Mudéjar additions. The proportions, however, have been extended here, and the exquisite elements of early Gothic take second place to the magnificence of the whole.

Feast your eyes, allowing them to roam around the enormous nave, seeking the upper panels of the altarpiece over the high altar, above the Classical-style altar of the trascoro. It has occasionally been proposed to raise this altar, leaving the *coro* (choir) open and offering the spectacle of a colossal nave without compare in the world, but the building was born in this way, and perhaps it is best, like the rose, not to touch it. Moreover, the *trascoro* is a sub-space with its own personality, for example, for the festivities of Corpus Christi, Holy Week and other lithurgical and cultural activities. Seville Cathedral, so enormous and well-proportioned, is, we might say, a «multi-church», allowing various celebrations to take place at the same time.

The nave is 16.24 metres wide, whilst the aisles have a width of 11 metres. In the original documentation which has survived, the height of the Cathedral is given in feet: 134 feet for the central nave, rising to 143 feet in the central dome, whilst the aisles reach a height of 96 feet, and the adjoining chapels 49 feet (figures from Ceán Bermúdez). The nave and aisles are each 126.18 metres in length.

The vaults are covered with four-sided elements, though those of the coro, the high chapel and the three central vaults of the transept take the form of a cross. The decoration of these central sections are so exquisite that Chueca Gointia likens them to the finest embroidery. In the original groundplan, the lantern was higher, similar in height to that of the Cathedral of Burgos, but it collapsed in 1511 and Juan Gil de Hontañón constructed the present dome, which is lower, its walls made lighter by the addition of windows.

In the centre of the *trascoro*, on the floor, is the tomb of Hernándo Colón, the cultivated son of Admiral Christopher Columbus, who bequeathed an important library to the Cathedral Chapter. The tomb is covered by a simple plaque in white marble, its

of Jerez de the Frontera. The side chapels are situated between the buttresses. All this represents the work of one hundred years, for the Cathedral was not blessed and officially opened until 11 May 1507, and many important elements were added once the basic fabric had been constructed. And still there are finishing touches to be made to certain ornamental motifs, such as the Puerta del Príncipe and of La Concepción. This circumstance has given rise to the popular saying that "this is going to take longer than building the Cathedral".

We should pause here to name the master builders who made the whole work possible: Alonso Martínez, original architect (1386-1396?); Pedro García (1421-1440); Igambret (1434); Carlín (1439-1449); Juan López (1443-1464); Juan Norman (1454-1472); Juan de Hoces (1478-1496); Simón de Colonia (1495-

inscription, which it is planned to restore, now almost illegible. The *trascoro* also contains the beautiful and complicated Baroque artefact (its main elements are displayed in other chapels) for the celebration of Corpus Christi. It is here that the Seises dance three times before the statue of the Santísimo, kept in the Custodia de Arfe. On that day, the *trascoro* becomes in itself a cathedral.

Until the 1960s, the Great Monument to Holy Thursday, made by Antonio Florentín between 1545 and 1554, was also exhibited in the centre of the *trascoro*. This was an enormous work in wood and paste with a base in the form of a Greek cross and a succession of niches formed by Doric, Ionic and Corinthian columns, decorated with sculptures by Gregorio Vázquez and other artists, crowned by a Calvary which can now be seen adjoining the upper section of the main doorway, where we are now. This Calvary almost touched the central vault. The head of Christ is by Ruiz Gijón, the author of El Cachorro. It was lighted by 120 silver lanterns and 441 candles, weighing 123 «arrobas» (units of 25 pounds) and 7 pounds of wax. It ceased to be displayed due to problems of restoring, though the Chapter still keeps the pieces in case one day it can be reconstructed. In its place, adjoining the interior of the doorway and covered with lavish velvet curtains is now the colossal silver Monument designed and constructed by Juan Laureano de Pina between 1770 and 1772.

Before leaving this area, we should approach the altar of the *trascoro*, opposite us. This is a richly-decorated piece in splendid marbles and jaspers, with bronze embellishments. Designed by Miguel de Zumárraga, it was built by Luis González between 1620 and 1634. On either side are marble reliefs depicting scenes from the Bible, as well as busts of the patron saints of Seville, Justa and Rufina. At the back are two doors leading up to the organs. Nevertheless, the most important element here is the painting of the Virgen de los Remedios, a panel painted by an anonymous early-15th century artist, much-restored, from the first overhaul, carried out in 1564 by Antón Pérez up to our times. It is now in a good state of preservation, however, and its serene, devout style reminds one of 14th-century paintings by members of the Sienna school.

Vault of the Cathedral crossing.

Altar of El Consuelo: painting of the Virgen del Consuelo with Child.

Altar of the Niño Mudo («Mute Child»): Baroque altarpiece.

An emotional and artistic pilgrimage

The characteristic which differentiates Seville Cathedral from all other similar edifices is that this cathedral is an enormous treasure trove containing numerous invaluable works from all orders of the fine and applied arts: altarpieces, paintings, sculptures, choirstalls, stained-glass windows, silverwork, grilles, ornaments, fabrics and choirbooks. A scholar would prefer to analyse this treasure by category, but for the occasional visitor it is recommended to follow a geographical itinerary, which is what we shall do in this guidebook. Prepare yourself for a remarkable emotional and artistic pilgrimage, then. Do not hurry: the visit can take an hour or two even without dawdling, but it is well worth the time spent.

Still in the *trascoro*, admire the chapels and altars on either side of the main entrance. Beginning with those on the left as we face the high altar, we find:

Altar del Consuelo: canvas on wood panel by Alonso Miguel de Tobar in 1720, representing the Virgen del Consuelo with the Child between Saint Anthony and Saint James. Notable influence of Murillo.

Altar del Niño Mudo: small 18th-century Baroque altarpice with a sculpture of Baby Jesus with tight-closed lips (hence the name of «Altar of the Mute Child»). Vainly attributed to Martínez Montañés, though executed in that artist's style. Fervently adored in Seville.

Chapel of San Leandro: rich, Baroque trefoiled portada, by Matías de Figueroa (1733-34). Excellent screen by Francisco Guzmán and De Ocampo the

Younger, completed in 1733. Inside the chapel the chapel, statues by Duque Cornejo, outstanding that of Saint Leander in the centre. On either side, Baroque paintings by Pedro de Uceda, disciple of Valdes Leal.

In the opening on the right of the entrance is a sculpture of the *Pietà*, known as the Virgen de la Alcobilla, 30 cm in height, Flemish in style and dating back to the late-15th-century.

Interior of the Puerta del Baptisterio and Altar de the

Visitación: behind a simple grille (1568), the Virgen Visiting Her Cousin Elizabeth, painted by Pedro Villegas Marmolejo (16th century), of Mannerist inspiration. Outstanding draftmanship and colouring of the clothes.

Chapel of Los Jácomes: founded by Flemish knights, its patrons are now the marquises of Tablantes. Plaster decoration on walls and ceiling. Outstanding painting of the *Pietà*, by Juan de Roelas (1609), recently restored.

Chapel of San Leandro: trefoiled doorway.

Chapel of San Leandro: painting of Saint Leander (Duque Cornejo).

Altar of the Angel de la Guarda, by Murillo.

Chapel of San Isidoro, identical to that of San Leandro, with similar portada, attributed to the same artists, and magnificent 18th-century grille. Plaster ornamentation also dating back to the 18th century. Inside, Baroque sculptures, presided over by the statue of Saint Isidoro.

Adjoining the chapel, the *Altar of the Virgen del Madroño,* a symphony of tender smiles attributed to Lorenzo Mercadante de Bretaña (1454), in polychromed stone. The Child ignores both the milk Mary is trying to give him and the berries the angel offers him. He only has eyes for you, the onlooker, smiling and blessing you. This is one of the most moving works in the Cathedral.

Altar of the Virgen de la Cinta: terracotta group, richly polychromed, also linked with Lorenzo Mercadante de Bretaña. The Virgin gives the Child a book to read. The Lady's cord gives this work its name. above is a painting of the Eternal Father, much revered in Seville.

On the other side of the Puerta de San Miguel is the *Altar del Nacimiento,* popularly known as the Chapel of La Providencia. Behind a Plateresque grille (1551), eight magnificent panels by Luis de Vargas, completed in 1555. The central theme is that of the Adoration of the Shepherds. This is a section of the Cathedral much revered in Seville: many come here to commend themselves to "Providence", without doubt through the offerings made here to the Child. Painted in Mannerist style, the central theme features exceptional movement and colour.

Before leaving the *trascoro*, raise your eyes to admire the wonderful colour of the stained-glass windows, of which there are a total of 81, ranging from the oldest, by Enrique Alemán in 1478, to those of the Chapel of San José, by the House of Maumejean, dating back to 1932. We will describe the different stained-glass windows over the course of our visit. Now look towards the main entrance. Over it, in the centre, is a large rose window depicting the four Evangelists, in large dimensions and strong colours: it is the work of the Mannerist artist Vicente Menardo in 1577, restored in 1831 (it needs restoration once more, but such work is never finished here). Also by

Opposite is an the elegant portada dating back to 1682, which communicates with the Parish Church of El Sagrario. All the patron saints of Seville are represented at the top: Saint Ferdinand in the centre, flanked by Saint Leandro and Saint Isidoro, and saints Justa and Rufina.

Let us turn now to the other side of the main entrance: *Altar of Angel de la Guarda,* adjoining the door itself. Here we find the first of the many Murillos in the Cathedral. Painted by Bartolomé Esteban between 1665 and 1669 for the Church of los Capuchinos, it was brought to the Cathedral in 1814. The work depicts a moving, tender scene, in soft colours and revealing splendid draftsmanship, with the light fully on the Child and backlighting featuring the elegantly-rendered angel.

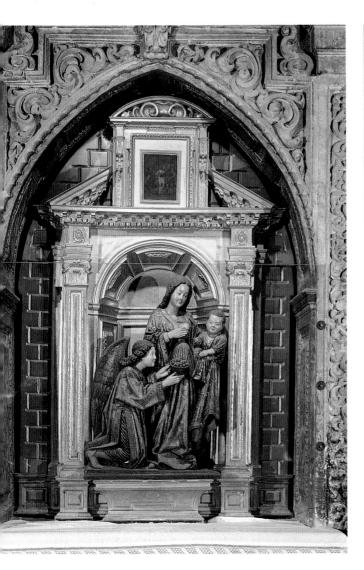

Altar of the Virgen del Madroño (Lorenzo Mercadante de Bretaña).

Altar of the Virgen de la Cinta.

Chapel of San Isidoro: painting of the saint.

Altar of El Nacimiento in the Chapel of Providencia (Luis de Vargas).

Menardo are the circular stained-glass windows over the Puerta del Baptisterio, the Visitation (1566) and over that of San Miguel, the Anunciation (1566). The two series of three on either side of the central nave of the *trascoro*, late-Gothic, are the oldest, and are all by Enrique Alemán between 1478 and 1483. On the south side are: Saint Peter, Saint Paul, Saint John the Evangelist and Saint John the Baptist; Jeroboam and other prophets; David, Isaiah, Daniel and Jeremiah. On the north side: Micheas, Abraham, Isaac and Amos; Abdias and other prophets; Daniel, Solomon, Habacuc and Methuselah.

Stained-glass window.

Rose window in the west wing of the nave.

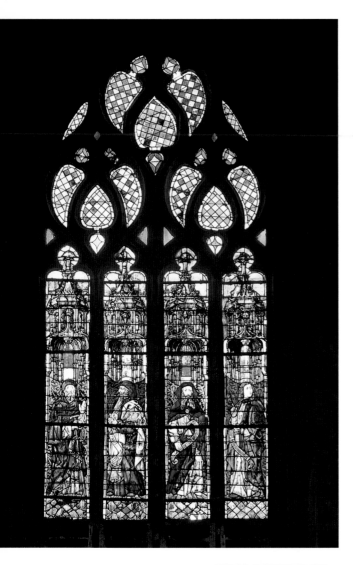

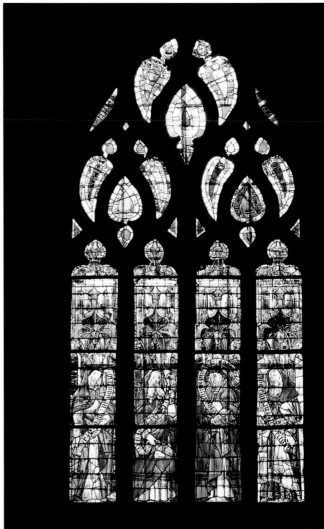

Stained-glass windows in the nave of the Trascoro.

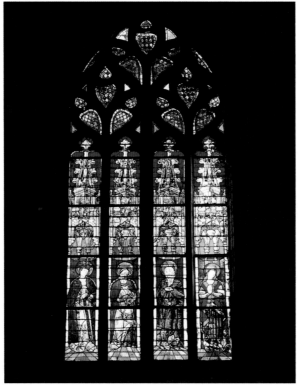

Stained-glass window.

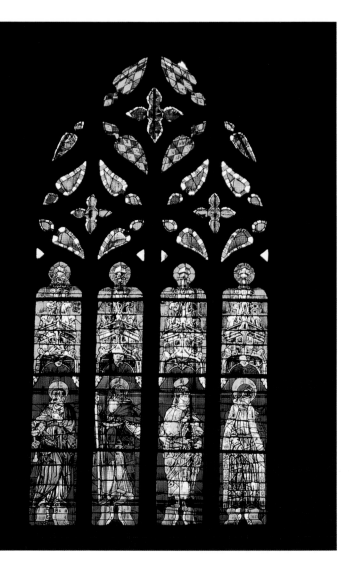

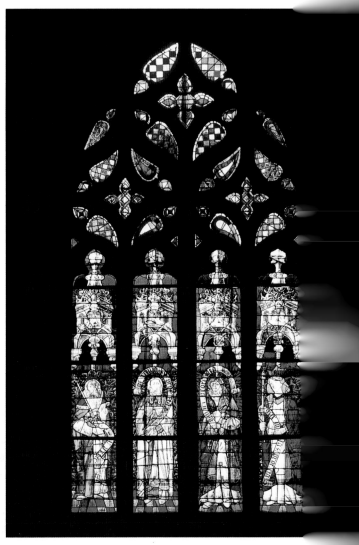

Stained-glass windows
in the nave of the
Trascoro.

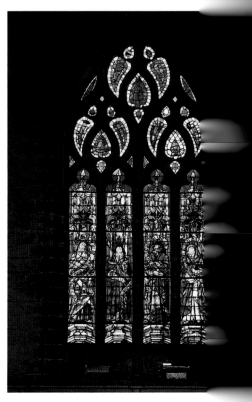

Stained-glass windows
in the nave.

Stained-glass windows
in the nave of the
Trascoro.

The aisles of the south side

From the interior of the Puerta of Saint Miguel, beginning at the Altar of the Providencia, described above, we shall take the following route:

Chapel of San Laureano: this is where, according to tradition, the building of the Cathedral fabric began. Grille dating back to 1702. Solomonic altarpiece (mid-18th century), with statue of San Laureano (one of the earliest prelates of the Sevillian Espicopacy) and reliefs illustrating the life of the saint. Some remains of frescoes by Lucas Valdés can still be seen on the walls. Tomb and statue at prayer of Cardinal Lluch (d. 1882), by Agapito Vallmitjana in 1885.

Upper stained-glass window: saints Catherine, Mary Magdalene, Martha and Margaret, by Enrique Alemán (1478-1479). Lower stained-glass window: saints Isidoro, Laureano and Leander, by Vicente Menardo (1572).

Chapel of El Cristo de Maracaibo: this chapel takes its name from the painting of the Christ of Maracaibo hanging there. The present work dates back to the 19th century and is a reproduction of another, now lost, dating back to the 18th century. The altarpiece was commissioned by the counts of Casa Galindo (whose burial-place is here) in 1914. Great local devotion is expressed in services for the redemption of souls. On the right, sepulchre of Cardinal de la Lastra, by Ricardo Bellver in 1880.

Chapel of San Laureano: tomb of Cardinal Lluch.

Chapel of El Cristo de Maracaibo: tomb of Cardinal Lastra.

Chapel of El Cristo de Maracaibo.

Chapel of El Cristo de Maracaibo: Altarpiece of San Bartolomé.

Upper and lower stained glass windows. Christ of Maracaibo Chapel.

Chapel of San José: Painting of the Wedding of Joseph and Mary (Valdés Leal).

But the most outstanding work in this chapel is the Altarpiece of San Bartolomé on the left, recently restored at the Chapter workshops. This is one of the oldest pieces in the Cathedral, and consists of 14 panels by early Sevillian artists. At the top is the Virgin with Child, a French Gothic-influenced work. The lower section formerly featured a painting of Saint Anna, an excellent copy of the original by Caracciolo in the Museum of Vienna. As this was extraneous to the original altarpiece, it has now been transferred elsewhere.

Upper stained-glass window: saints Agatha, Lucy, Cecilia and Ines, by Enrique Alemán (1478-1479). Lower stained-glass window: Holy Family (1797). On the walls, various 17th-century paintings.

Chapel of San José: the altarpiece, left, is Neo-Classical, in marble and jasper, finely executed by José Estévez. Opposite the altarpiece is the tomb of Cardinal Joaquín Tarancón (d. 1862). Over the tomb is a painting of the Wedding of Joseph and Mary, by Valdés Leal in 1667. Other paintings in this chapel: Saint Justa and Saint Rufina, Seville School (17th century), inspired by models by Zurbarán; The Sacrifice of Isaac and the Adultress, attributed to the Venetian circle of the Bassanos; two half-length paintings of Apostles, Seville School (17th century); Biblical scene, Flemish School, also 17th century; Investiture of Saint Ildephonse.

Upper stained-glass window: saints Gregory, Augustine, Ambrose and Jerome, by Enrique Alemán (1478-1479). Lower stained-glass window: Adoration of the Shepherds, inspired by the panel by Luis de Vargas in the Chapel of "La Providencia", made in the Maumejean workshops in Madrid in 1932; crowning it, the Saint Blas from the stained-glass window which formerly existed here. Below this window, the engraved tombstone of Cardinal Bueno Monreal, last deceased archbishop of Seville (d. 1987), relief in bronze by José Antonio Márquez of Aracena.

Chapel of San Hermenegildo: the most interesting element here is the tomb of Cardinal Juan de Cervantes (d. 1453), an outstanding theologist and papal legate at the Council of Basle in 1437, and who donated this chapel. The tomb is in alabaster, a magnificent example of Sevillian Gothic art by Lorenzo Mercadante de Bretaña (1458): pure filigree the entire work, with startling realism of the recumbent figure, whose head seems truly to press into the three pillows on which it rests. At the base are angels reminiscent of the style of Van Eyck, sustaining the coat of arms of the Cervantes; another deer, symbol of that family, lies at the feet of the prelate. This is,

Chapel of San José: stained-glass windows.

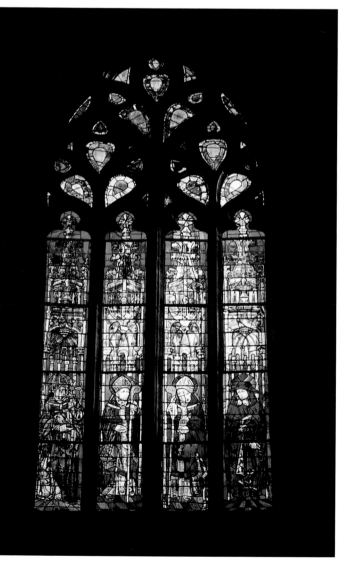

Chapel of San Hermenegildo: Saint James the Younger.

Chapel of San Hermenegildo: sculpture of Saint James the Elder.

without a doubt, the finest tomb in Seville Cathedral. The statue of Saint Hermenegild (on the left) is by the Sevillian artist Bartolomé García de Santiago, and dates back to the early-18th century. His son, Manuel, carved the altarpiece. On either side of the altar, two interesting sculptures: James the Elder in pilgrim's dress, an anonymous 16th-century piece in polychromed wood, and James the Younger, in poly- chromed stone, attributed to Pedro Millán (1500), the only piece salvaged from the lantern when it col- lapsed in 1511.

To the right of the chapel is a tomb containing the remains of the High Admiral of Castile Juan Mate de Luna (d. 1337). Paintings in the chapel: Immaculate Conception, attributed to Juan Roelas; saints Engracia and Rufina, attributed to the Sevillian artist Bernabé de Ayala (17th century), copy of the Virgen de la Antigua; the Wedding of Canaan, and Salomé with the Head of John the Baptist, Flemish School (17th century), and Saint Liberata, local school, also painted in the 17th century.

Upper stained-glass window: four bishops, by Enrique Alemán (1478-1479). Lower stained-glass window: Saint Hermenegild, in a long niche terminating in a pointed arch, dating back to the year 1819.

Chapel of the Virgen de la Antigua: the most impor- tant of the minor chapels, a church within a church, constantly altered and extended over the years the chapel was completely restored recently, the work being finished in 1991, in preparation for the celebra- tions of 1992, as the Virgen de la Antigua, which presides the chapel, is much worshipped not just in

Chapel of San Hermenegildo: tomb of Juan de Cervantes (Lorenzo Mercadante de Bretaña).

Chapel of San Hermenegildo: statue of Saint Hermenegildo (García de Santiago).

Chapel of San Hermenegildo: tomb of Admiral Mayor de Castilla Mate de Luna.

Chapel of the Virgen de la Antigua: al fresco painting.

Chapel of the Virgen de la Antigua: tomb of Cardinal Diego Hurtado de Mendoza.

Seville, but also in many regions of South America. The Virgen de la Antigua was present in the old church-mosque (hence her name, to the referring to her antiquity), painted on a wall in the place now occupied by the entrance grille, looking into the chapel. The painting was transferred to its present site in 1578, under the direction of the architect Asencio de Maeda. This is a delicate al fresco painting, larger than life, containing certain traces of Byzantine iconography. According to legend, Saint Ferdinand managed to enter Seville one night before it was reconquered, and prayed before this Virgin. It was the Saint himself who later decided where the work should be placed in the cathedral-mosque. The Virgin holds a rose in her right hand, whilst the Child holds a small bird. Three angels are in attendance at

the top. Between the two at the bottom is the crown in relief with which the image was canonised by Cardinall lundain on 24 November 1929, coinciding with the Iberoamerican Exhibition in Seville. Both this crown and that worn by the Child are made of gold and precious stones, paid for by popular subscription and made at the Granda workshops in Madrid. At the foot of the statue is a woman praying, identified by Ceán Bermúdez as Doña Leonor, wife of Don Fernando de Antequera.

The chapel was extended between 1495 and 1504, when the Cardinal Archbishop of Seville, Diego Hurtado de Mendoza, chose it as his burial-place. The ribbed vaults are in Late-Gothic style. The grille, begun by Fray Francisco of Salamanca in 1530, was completed by Juan López of Granada at the end of

Altarpiece in the Chapel of the Virgen de la Antigua. ▷

Chapel of the Virgen de la Antigua: silver lampstand.

Chapel of the Virgen de la Antigua: ebony door.

Chapel of the Virgen de la Antigua: the Tabernacle.

the 16th century, under the direction of Hernán Ruiz (author of the upper section of the Giralda). The interior stained-glass window replaces an earlier window in Renaissance style, lost in the 18th century. The present window represents Saint Ferdinand enthroned, and is by the House of Zettler, Munich in the late-19th century, after a design by José Gestoso.

On the left, the magnificent Renaissance tomb of Cardinal Diego Hurtado de Mendoza, carved in Genoa by Domenico Fancelli de Setignano, who came to Seville to install it in 1510. It is conceived in the form of a triumphal arch. Opposite is something like a replica of the tomb by Pedro Duque Cornejo and in which Archbishop Luis de Salcedo y Azcona received burial in 1741.

The chapel contains one hundred other artistic marvels. On its walls are 21 paintings by the Sevillian artist Domingo Martínez (18th century). Over the altar, a magnificent ivory crucifix by Cortezo. Silver candelabra by Hernández de Ballesteros (16th century); silver communion rail and large lamps, also silver, handing from bronze supports. The altarpiece

containing the Virgen de the Antigua is in fine marble and was donated by Salcedo y Azcona. It was completed in 1738 by Juan Fernández de Iglesias and is adorned by ten statues in white marble by Duque Cornejo. The tabernacle, in jasper, silver and gold and enamel, is crowned by a statue of Saint Joseph. Magnificent door on the right of the altar, communicating with the sacristy and made of ebony incrusted with tortoiseshell and bronze. The sacristy is now used for Chapter meetings, and is closed to the public. It contains, amongst other splendid works of art, six excellent 18th-century works in copper (restored) of the Flemish School featuring scenes from the life of the Virgin. It is a tradition for the flags of the Iberoamerican countries to hang in this chapel.

Finally, outside is a superb Renaissance portal communicating the chapel with the transept, completed in around 1570 by Juan López. The two green marble columns which flank it formerly supported the pulpits of the Cathedral. Among the many personages buried in this chapel is the musician Francisco Guerrero.

Chapel of the Virgen de la Antigua: Renaissance grille. ▷

Chapels of the Alabasters: grilles.

The "Sancta Sanctorum" of the art of Seville Cathedral

With the visit to the Chapel of La Virgen de la Antigua we enter the heart or "sancta sanctorum" of the artistic treasures contained in Seville Cathedral. On leaving this chapel, turn back the way you came to approach the two twin chapels opposite, in the inner aisles, under the upper passage of the organ in this aisle. These chapels, along with two more identical to them in the opposite aisles, are known as the Chapels of Los Alabastros.

They were designed by Diego de Riaño and constructed between 1531 and 1554, with Gothic ornamentation. The two highly decorative grilles date back to the 17th century. Between them is a Virgin and Child in polychrome alabaster (73 cm), known as

the Virgin of Genoa, as some of these works came from that Italian city.

The Chapel of La Inmaculada Concepción, on the right, is a delight. Here is the intensely moving, serenely dynamic, transcendentally spiritual «Cieguecita», the Immaculate, one of the three masterpieces of Martínez Montañés, of which Villar Movellán said, on its completion in 1631, that it was spoken of as "the first thing to be made in the world". All in her is beauty and balance, from the tender little heads of the angels supporting it to the soft appearance of the polychromed robes, the stylised fingers of the joined hands, the neck, like that of a Greek goddess, the face of the Virgin, servant of the Lord, the humble eyes of «the little blind one», the pure forehead and the lovely long hair tumbling down. The people of Seville are proud to be able to admire her beauty

Chapels of the Alabasters: statue of the Immaculate, «La Cieguecita», by Montañés.

continually. This is a Virgin to pray to -pray to her if you will- and no Sevillian passes before her without uttering the classical "Ave, María Purísima". The altarpiece was also carved by Martínez Montañés and was polychromed by Francisco Pacheco, who painted the donors, bequeathing to history the likeness of Francisco Gutiérrez de Molina and his wife Jerónima de Zamudio, who made this prodigy of art possible. Take your time, for the tourist lives few such moments of extasy.

On the left is the *Chapel of La Encarnación,* whose altarpiece represents the moment of the Annunciation. All its figures are finely depicted and reveal the influence of Montañés. The altarpiece was completed between 1630 and 1635.

To the right of the Chapel of "La Cieguecita", the arches give acess to the Coro, in rich red jasper and Baroque coffering. The doors (the one on the left is false) are by Luis de Vilches in 1730 and are made of dark ebony, plated in polished copper.

Chapels of the Alabasters: Altarpiece of the Annunciation.

Chapels of the Alabasters: statue of the Virgin of Genoa.

Altar of the trascoro.

The nave and crossing. ▷

Capilla Mayor and Coro

Stand in the centre of the transept, opposite the entrance to the high altar, separated from the nave by the majestic Renaissance grille in gilded bronze, the work of the Dominican Francisco de Salamanca between 1518 and 1529. This artist also completed the splendid pulpits in 1532.

When Pope John Paul II visited the Cathedral on 5 November 1982, tears came into his eyes as he raised them towards the high altarpiece, which is an extraordinary work: besides being the largest in the Christian world, measuring 20 metres high by 18 wide, it constitutes an impressive, harmonious forest of magnificent carvings and other works of art. It transpires mysticism, like an open book telling the life

of Christ in 28 niches, separated by a mesh of pilasters, ledges, daises, between which are distributed 189 minor sculptures. Outstanding are the four central scenes representing the Nativity, the Assumption of Mary (to whom the Cathedral is devoted), the Resurrection and the Ascension of the Lord. The frieze below depicts scenes from the religious history of Seville. Above, jutting out in the form of a baldachin, is the «viga» (beam) presided over by the magnificent Pietà, jutting out in the form of a canopy, the "viga", presidida por magnífica Piedad and on either side the 12 Apostles, the entire piece crowned by a wonderful Gothic Calvary, whose figure is known as the "Cristo del Millón" (after the million indulgences this Christ is said to have granted).

Over the altar is the huge silver Tabernacle, by Fran-

Altar of the trascoro: panel of the Virgen de los Remedios.

cisco de Alfaro (1593-1596), on a pedastal by Luis de Acosta and partially gilded by Laureano de Pina (1688). Over it is the lovely Virgen de La Sede, donated by Alphonse X, the Virgin with Child, patron saint of the Cathedral, carved in cypress wood and silver plated, a French-Gothic-inspired work dating back to the 13th century.

A curious anecdote: the lower sections of the outer rows (somewhat deteriorated) contain representations of two personages linked with the origins of Seville: Hercules and Julius Cesar, founder (according to legend) and Romaniser, respectively, of the city.

The altarpiece is carved in a variety of woods (larch, pine, chestnut, etc), all gilded and polychromed. This is, fundamentally, a Gothic work, though the sides are in Renaissance style. The Flemish artist Pyeter Dancart began work on it in 1482, and he was succeeded by Jorge Fernández Alemán, Alejo Fernández, Roque de Balduque and Juan Bautista Vázquez, who completed the altarpiece in 1564. The Capilla Mayor is enclosed on either side by two Renaissance grilles (1518-1522), by Sancho Muñoz, Juan de Yepes, Maestro Esteban, Diego de Huidobro and Juan de Conillana. Over them, on the right and left, are stained-glass windows featuring the Dormition and Glorification of the Virgin, by Juan Jacques between 1511 and 1518.

The altarpiece was recently cleaned and restored and is now in excellent condition. The entire piece is transfigured when the great religious offices are celebrated in this Cathedral, most especially those of Holy Week and the Immaculate Conception. In the presbytery below dance the famous Seises in the octaves of Corpus Christi (dressed in white and red) and the Immaculate (in white and light blue). The Seises also danced for Pope John Paul II, though not here, but before the altar installed in the grounds of Seville Fair for the beatification of Sor Angela de la Cruz.

Tear yourself away from the wonder of the high altar and turn to admire another jewel, the Coro, separated

Coro: Grille of Fray Francisco de Salamanca (16th century).

Overall view of the coro.

Coro: lectern.

Coro: statue of the Virgin and Child.

Capilla Mayor: statue of the Virgen de la Sede (13th century).

Capilla Mayor: tabernacle.

from the nave by another colossal grille by Fray Francisco de Salamanca (1518-1523). We remind you that the pillar on the left was demolished in 1888, but work carried out under the skilled direction of José Gestoso restored things to their correct state. The Coro occupies a space measuring 20 metres by 14. The choir stalls, in ebony for the most part, are in Gothic-Mudéjar style, and are unique in the world. They consist of 67 high chairs with baldachin and 50 low seats. The King's Seat bears the royal coat of arms and the following inscription: "Este coro fizo Nufro Sanchez entallador que Dios aya acabose año de 1478". Besides the mentioned artist, Pyeter Dancart, Gonzalo Gómez, Horozco and Diego Guillén also worked on it, however.

At the rear, in the centre, is the archbishop's seat, crowned with high Gothic pinnacles. Throughout the stalls are rich carvings representing scenes from the Old and New testaments. The backs of the lower chairs are adorned with representations of the Giralda, those of the upper stalls with Mudéjar inlaying. These are separated by small columns with saints. In the centre of the Coro are various furnishings, outstanding being the lectern, completed between 1562 and 1565 by the sculptors Juan Marín, Bautista Vázquez and Francisco Hernández. The reliefs were cast by Bartolomé Morel. It consists of two sections, the lower part revolving to facilitate use of the large old choirbooks. In a kiosk above is a splendid figure of the Virgin and Child by Bautista Vázquez. The lectern

Capilla Mayor: altarpiece. ▷

Capilla Mayor and Grille of Fray Francisco de Salamanca (16th century).

Columns of the transept.

Dance of the Seises.

is crowned by a crucifix and the Four Evangelists. There are two independent organs here, on either side of the Coro, though the two can be coupled and played from the central console (first section of the Coro). This console consists of four manual keyboards and a large pedalier. Over the centuries, various organ systems have been used, all of them excellent. The current Romantic systems are by Aquilino Amezúa between 1901 and 1903. The electronic system was adopted in 1973, when the console was also lowered so that the organs could be used for large concerts, including concerts involving orchestras. The rich tones of its «swells» are impressive, and its more delicate registers, such as «vox humana» and «vox celeste» highly moving. There are some splendid recordings available on record and cassette by the Cathedral's current organist, Enrique Ayarra. The two cases, on either side, containing the tubes, date back to the 18th century and correspond to the design by Luis Vilches, with sculptures by Duque Cornejo. The Coro was completed restored some years ago, through the munificence of the *Real Maestranza de Caballería* of Seville, an association with close fraternal ties with the Cathedral Chapter, its members having seats in the Coro itself.

There is also a magnificent example of an English chamber organ, built by Gabriel Buntebart in 1787 and acquired by the chapter in 1801. According to the organist José Enrique Ayarra, only ten instruments like this are known to exist in the world, of which the only one that continues in use is this one. It accompanies services in the *Antigua* chapel, where it can be seen here in the foreground.

Stained-glass windows in the Coro: north side (right), the furthest away is by Enrique Alemán (1478-1483), and represents Manasseh, Ananias, Jeroboam and Josaphat; the nearer one, by Arnao de Vergara (1535), depicts Tobias, Zacharias, Balaam and Jonah; south side (left), furthest away, Hosea, Abraham, Elias and Aaron, by Enrique Alemán (1478-1483); the window nearest us was replaced by the House of Zettler in 1908 after the collapse of the transept column mentioned above. The model followed was that of the

Vault in the coro.

North wing of the transept. ▷

Coro: console of the organs.

Organ of the Epistle. ▷

original, by Arnao de Vergara in 1535, and represents Isaiah, Jeremiah, Ezequiel and Daniel.

The stained-glass windows on the four sides of the transept follow a similar pattern. The two above the grille and on the north side are by Arnao de Vergara (1525-1526), that at the rear representing the Presentation of the Virgin in the Temple, the Annunciation and the Visitation, whilst that of the north side features scenes relating to Jesus in the Temple with the Learned Men. The present windows above the grille of the Coro and on the south side are reproductions of the orginals, by the House of Zettler in 1913, and contain scenes from the secret life of Jesus.

Let us now turn our gaze to the south side of the transept, in which we find, in the foreground, the tomb of Admiral Christopher Columbus. These are

the remains of Columbus which have always been considered authentic, and were kept first in Santo Domingo and, when part of the island of Haiti (the Spanish area) passed into French hands by virtue of the 1795 Treaty of Basle, were transferred to the Isle of Cuba, then a Spanish possession. When Cuba became independent in 1898, the Discoverer's remains were brought to Seville in the royal yacht "Giralda", which sailed up the Guadalquivir on 19 January 1899. They were deposited by order of the Spanish government in a mausoleum designed by Arturo Mélida in 1891, the deposit being added in 1902. The coffin is seen being carried by the kings of arms, in bronze, of the four original reigns of Spain: Castile, Leon, Aragon and Navarre.

In 1877, a new «discovery» of the remains of Columbus

Tomb of Christopher Columbus.

Painting of Saint Christopher, by Pérez de Alesio.

was orchestrated in Santo Domingo, not only placing in doubt those kept peacefully for years in Seville, but also itself leaving room for serious doubt. A well-documented study of the controversy by Manuel Ballesteros is "Los restos de Cristóbal Colón en la Catedral de Sevilla", to be found in the book "La Catedral de Sevilla", Ediciones Guadalquivir, pp. 801 ff. Behind the Mausoleum of Columbus are some highly interesting paintings: on the right as we look, in the Chapel and Altar of la Concepción, a splendid canvas by Luis de Vargas featuring, in the foreground, the figures of Adam, nude, in magnificent foreshortening, and Eve, dressed. This chapel is popularly known as "La Gamba" («the prawn»), in allusion to an anecdote which has been passed down from generation to generation: "gamba" in Italian, means «leg», and it is

said that, after Luis de Vargas had completed the painting of Adam's leg, the Italian Mateo Pérez de Alesio, who was working on the nearby Mural of Saint Cristóbal (left side), said: "Piu vale la tua gamba che il mio tutto San Cristóforo" ('your «leg» is worth more than the whole of my Saint Christopher'). The Altar of "La Gamba" was completed in 1561.

The Mural of Saint Cristóbal, for its part, is by Pérez de Alesio in 1584. It is a magnificent example of this type of painting, typical of Spanish cathedrals. In it, Saint Christopher is depicted helping the Child over a river. The work, whose use of colour is outstanding, was recently restored.

On the other side of the door (left), is another magnificent chapel, this one containing a painting of the *Pietà*, to which two artists contributed their considerable skills: the three central figures (Christ, Mary and Mary Magdalene) are by Alejo Fernández, whilst the figures in the background are attributed to Pedro Fernández de Guadalupe. The painting is dated 1527 and was also recently restored.

Both chapels contain magnificent Renaissance grilles (16th century).

The collection of stained-glass windows on this side of the transept are the most decorative in the entire Cathedral, and appear as if they were embroidered in glass. All are by Arnao de Flandes (1548-1556), except the central rose window, representing the Assumption of Mary, by Arnao de Vergara (1536), and that over the side door of the Chapel of La Antigua, by the House of Maumejean between 1929 and 1932 and representing figures of saints.

Under the rose window of the Assumption is a magnificent neo-classical clock, still in use, dating back to the year 1789 and the work of Manuel Núñez and Fray José Cordero. This clock governs the organisation of time within the Cathedral.

Southern aisle and crossing.

Altar of La Piedad.

Chapel of La Concepción («La Gamba»): painting of Adam and Eve by Luis de Vargas.

Chapel of Los Dolores: painting of Jacob Blessing his Children.

Approaching the Cathedral museums

The Chapter plans to construct a large art gallery, the design of which has already been drawn up by the Cathedral Master of the Fabric, Alfonso Jiménez, to make known the huge collection of works of arts contained in the Cathedral. This could be the second-largest art museum in Spain, after the Prado. At present, many of the pieces are housed in dependencies of the Chapter, closed to the general public.

It is also true that, after Expo'92 Seville, all guides to the Cathedral have become out of date, for on that occasion, the Cathedral was converted into the city's pavilion, containing the impressive «Magna Hispalensis» collection, after which important event the organisation of the Cathedral Treasures is vastly changed. And that is not all, for many paintings have been taken to the repair workshop, and are being distributed among various chapels according to the conventional criteria of the Cathedral Services. Our guide contains the most up-to-date itinerary, however, but do not be surprised if you find the occasional empty niche or space awaiting the return of a work under restoration.

Leaving behind the south side of the transept, we come, on the right, to the *Chapel of los Dolores*, entrance to the first large museum area, that known as the Sacristy of los Cálices. The chapel is presided over by a Baroque altarpiece with a 16th-century crucifix and a fine half-length Virgen de los Dolores by

Chapel of Los Dolores: Baroque altarpiece.

Chapel of Los Dolores: tomb of Cardinal Spinola.

Pedro de Mena, dating back to the second half of the 17th century. Opposite is the great *Tenebrario*, recently installed here, though it is considered that it could be seen to greater effect in the Sacristía Mayor. This figure, carved in bronze and wood between 1559 and 1562, measures 7.80 metres in height. It is thought to have been designed by Hernán Ruiz and cast by Bartolomé Monreal, with the help of Pedro Delgado. The models for the sculptures are by Juan Bautista Vázquez the Elder, Juan Giralte and Juan Martín. The base has a rotary system, as it used to be carried to the grille of the high altar on Easter Thursday and Good Friday. The triangle at the top has supports for the fifteen candles which were extinguished at each Psalm of the matins and laudes

services, the central candle corresponding to the «Miserere», of great tradition in these offices.

At the rear of the chapel is the tomb of Cardinal Marcelo Spínola y Maestre (died in 1906), prelate of great virtue, beatified in Rome by Pope John Paul II on 29 March 1987. This is a fine work by Joaquín Bilbao. Small interior stained-glass window with the coat of arms of Cardinal Ilundain, made in 1931.

Some fine paintings are also contained in this chapel: the Tenebrist *Ecce homo*, attributed to Alonso Cano; The Transfer of Christ to the Tomb, according to some reminiscent of the studio of Caravaggio, whilst others attribute the work to the French artist Bigot; Denial of Saint Peter, French School though with touches reminiscent of Velazquez; and Jacob Blessing his Children, reminiscent of the style of Diepen Beek.

From this chapel we pass through into the first museum room, known as the *Sacristy of los Cálices.* Built of stone, with three late-Gothic vaults, plain and highly elegant, this was started by Diego de Riaño and terminated by Martín de Gaínza in 1534. The Sacristy contains a small but priceless art collection. At the rear is a large painting of the patron saints of Seville, Justa and Rufina, by Francisco de Goya y Lucientes (1817), commissioned by the Cathedral Chapter for this site. The saints wear dress typical of the work of Goya, with rudely beautiful faces, the background featuring a Sevillian landscape.

The paintings on the left wall as we look at that of Saints Justa and Rufina are as follows: Saint Peter in Pontifical Robes (first half of the 16th century), by Pedro Fernández de Guadalupe; four large, interest-

Sacristy of the Chalices.

Cristo de la Clemencia by Martínez Montañés (Chapel of San Andrés).

Sacristía Mayor.

ing panels painted by Alejo Fernández in 1508: Presentation of the Child at the Temple; Birth of the Virgin; Meeting of Joachim and Anne; and the Adoration of the Magi, exceptional pieces combining highly expressive figures with achronic architectural elements and everyday domestic utensils. In the corner is a restored panel (15th century) by Juan Sánchez de Castro, representing the Virgin with Saint Peter and Saint Jerome.

On the other side, from the entrance door: Saint Anne with the Virgin and Child by Caracciolo (17th century); Saint John the Baptist, by Zurbarán, around 1640; Saint Peter being Freed by the Angel, by Zurbarán around 1656; the Holy Trinity, by Luis Tristán, a disciple of El Greco, dated 1624; Calvary, by Juan Sánchez III, (15th

century); The Gloria, by Roelas (17th century); Adoration of the Magi, by Jacobo Jordaens, dating back to the year 1669; Virgin of the Rosary, studio of Zurbarán; Guardian Angel, by Mattia Preti (17th century); The Piety, with Saint Vincent, Saint Michael and donor, late-15th century anonymous panel; Saint Lazarus with Martha and Mary, by Valdés Leal, around 1658; The Circumcision, by Jacobo Jordaens in 1669; and Saint Jerome, by Pablo Legot (18th century). At the moment of writing this guide there were two empty spaces at on either side of the picture by Goya, awaiting the restoration of the *Ecce Homo,* a triptych by Luis de Morales in around 1650 and a painting of Mary Magdalene by Artemisa Gentillegi (17th century), at present in the Mayordomía.

Vault of the Sacristía
Mayor.

Sacristía Mayor: Saint
Ferdinand, a sculpture by
Roldán.

Sacristía Mayor: statue of
the Virgin by Alonso
Martínez.

Sacristía Mayor: Saint Leander (Murillo).

Sacristía Mayor: Saint Isidoro (Murillo).

At the rear are two oratories, that of the Virgen del Rosario (relief), with irvory crucifix, attributed to Alonso Cano and 16th-century ceremonial salver; and Saint Francis of Paula, a painting Zurbarán, with another irvory crucifix and 18th-century salvers.

In the cabinets on either side is exhibited a priceless collection of sacred cups. Outstanding is the golden chalice donated by Cardinal Delgado y Venegas in 1777; and another one, also in gold with blue enamel, a gift from Isabel II; and the reliquary of Saint Millan de la Cogolla, a Mexican piece made in 1578, donated by Canon Mateos Gago.

The Chapel of San Andrés, which used to be presided over by a painting of the Martyrdom of Saint Andrew, now top right, a mediocre copy of the original by Roelas. The chapel is now a bizarre place ornamentally speaking, breaking with the natural air of the other chapels of the Cathedral. Heavy, ostentatious crimson hangings conceal the neo-Gothic altarpiece, formerly presided over by the statue of the Sacred Heart, carved in Barcelona by Claudio Rius and which Cardinal Segura ordered to be placed here during the 1940s. Below a baldachin is the splendid statue of the Christ of Clemency, a masterpiece by Martínez Montañés commissioned by Canon Vázquez de Leca in 1603 for his oratory. It was later placed in the Charterhouse of Las Cuevas and was acquired by the Chapter when this monastery was disentailed in the 19th century. The statue was placed in the Sacristy of los Cálices (for which reason it is also known as the Christ of the Chalices) in the space now occupied by Goya's portrayal of saints Justa and Rufina. It was loaned by the Chapter to the Vatican's pavilion during the Universal Exhibition Seville'92, at the end of which it was installed here. An academicist work, it is also tender, harmonious, its feet crossed. In spite of its poor present installation, it is worth taking some time to admire. On its right is the lovely statue of the Virgen del Buen Aire, which was displayed in the «Magna Hispalensis» Exhibition in 1992. It was at first a high relief, carved by Juan de Oviedo in 1700 for the Triana nautical school, being trans-ferred subsequently to the seat of the same institution in the Palacio de Saint Telmo and finally given complete form by Duque Cornejo mid-way through the 18th century. The statue, with little boat to the right and the Child on the left, is a delight, but a further blunder has been made by placing it next to the Christ of Clemency, as, being so different one from another, they clash. The statue of the Sacred Heart (greatly missed by some worshippers) was taken to the adjoining Parish Church of El Sagrario and placed in an altarpiece of jasper which does not suit it at all. To accommodate this change, continuing the chain of

Sacristía Mayor: Saint Martha and Mary Magdalene, by Valdés Leal.

Sacristía Mayor: Pietà by Francisco Bayeu.

Sacristía Mayor: Panel of the Descent (Pedro de Campaña).

folly, the crucifix which had been made for it was removed.

On the right of the chapel are the tombs of the Pérez de Guzmán y Ayala family, whose main interest resides in their age. On the walls are two huge paintings by the Napolitan artist Lucas Jordán (1632-1702), representing the transfer of the Arc of the Covenant and the Song of Deborah. Over the grille is a stained-glass window depicting the Last Supper, by Arnao de Flandes (1555).

We now enter the Sacristia Mayor, used as such only on Easter Thursday. This is the largest museum space in the Cathedral. In the atrium on the right is a glass cabinet containing a fine example of the many old choirbooks possessed by the Cathedral. The higher stained-glass window is by Arnao de Flandes (1566), and features the Expulsion of the Merchants from the Temple. On either side are large cupboards carved by Duque Cornejo (1743). At the end is an interesting painting of Saint Anthony of Padua, by the studio of Zurbarán.

Of such colossal dimensions is the Sacristy that Philip II is said to have said to the canons on seeing it that, «You have a better Sacristy than I a church». Crossing its Plateresque entrance and passing under an oblique arch, we discover a space rich in ornament, beginning with the doors, carved by Diego Guillén in 1548. The entire room is a splendid Renaissance-Plateresque monument. Work began on it in 1532 under the direction of Diego de Riaño, with the co-operation of Diego de Siloé and Hernán Ruiz. It was completed by Martín de Gainza in 1543. The groundplan is in the form of a Greek cross, its arms short and with chamfered angles, 18 metres in length and 33 metres in height. Other elements are: columns of compound orders; arms covered by fan vaults; half-orange dome, richly adorned and crowned by a lantern, which, with the four oculi shed bright sunlight into the room.

At the rear are three splendid inter-communicating chapels. In the central of the three, decorated with reliefs of the Assumption, is a work greatly admired due to its composition, movement and colour: The Descension, an oil on panel produced in 1548 by Pedro de Campaña and acquired by the Chapter in 1814 from the demolished Parish Church of Santa Cruz. In the chapel on the left as we face it are: an anonymous painting of the Martyrdom of Saint Lawrence (17th century). More interesting is the canvas hanging in the chapel on the right, a portrait of Saint Theresa by the studio of Zurbarán (between 1641 and 1658). Of the statues of the Child Jesus in the central

Sacristía Mayor: portrait of Saint Theresa (studio of Zurbarán).

Sacristy of the Chalices: Saints Justa and Rufina, by Goya.

Sacristía Mayor: carved doors (1498).

Sacristy of the Chalices: Birth of Mary, by Alejo Fernández.

chapel, the most interesting is the Baroque full-length piece attributed to La Roldana. On the left, a marvellous head of Saint John the Baptist, by Juan de Mesa (17th century) on from Limoges.

The paintings hanging on the walls, beginning with the head, right, by the door as we enter, are: The Piety, by Francisco Bayeu of Saragossa, signed 1788; The Vision of Saint Francis, by Sánchez Cotán (17th century); Saint Leandro, one of the most famous works of Bartolomé Esteban Murillo (that of Saint Isidoro is opposite); and Our Lady of Mercy, by de Roela (around 1621). On the other side is a space for an Inmaculada, by an anonymous 16th-century Sevillian artist, currently being restored. Next is Saint Isidoro by Murillo; The Apparition of Christ to Saint Ignatius of Loyola, by Alonso Vázquez (around 1595);

and Saints Justa and Rufina, by the Sevillian artist Miguel de Esquivel (around 1620).

Sculptures: on the right of the entrance: Saint Ferdinand, by Pedro Roldán in 1671; and, on the left, Inmaculate Conception, by Alonso Martínez in 1658, both of which are carried in the Corpus Christi procession.

Silverwork: before all and above all, the huge Monstrance for the Corpus, by Juan de Arfe between 1580 and 1587. This is one of the most famous works by Arfe, and is a model of Plateresque art. In 1668, Juan de Segura removed the statue of Faith in the first section, replacing it with a figure representing the Immaculate, a theme much associated with the Sevillian eucharistic tradition. The monstrance measures 3.25 metres in height and weighs 300 kilos. It has

four sections and features 24 columns of the Ionic, Corinthian and compound orders. It is adorned with small figures of Fathers of the Church and illustrious theologians. In the second section, for the Corpus procession, is placed the small monstrance for the Holy Sacrament, by Thamaral (exhibited in another room).

The Sacristy contains four glass display cabinets. The first, on the right, contains a collection of 17th-century reliquaries and a *Lignum Crucis,* with the burial group of Christ, a beautiful work dating back to the 14th century and donated by Cardinal Gómez de Albornoz in 1389, restored in 1605 by Lázaro Hernández Rincón. In the second cabinet are displayed a number of lithurgical ornaments, changed for reasons of conservation. However, outstanding is the water ewer of La Sierpe, of gilded silver and finely embossed, and two urns for sacred oils, made in Antwerp in the 16th century. These three pieces were acquired by the Chapter in 1564 from the Bishop's Chamber in Burgos.

On the left, in the first cabinet, is a collection of 16th-century gilded silver urn-reliquaries, as well as gem-encrusted pectoral crosses and rings, but the outstanding item displayed here is the *Lignum Crucis* with the golden pectoral cross of Pope Clement XIV which the Chapter commissioned Antonio Méndez to make in 1796: the cross rests on a globe of the earth held by angels and on which is engraved the *mapa mundi.*

In the second cabinet is an exceptional piece, considered one of the outstanding works of Spanish Gothic silverwork. These are the so-called *Tablas Alfonsíes*, a reliquary commissioned by King Alphonse X, the Wise, for his oratory, and which he bequeathed to Seville Cathedral in his testamentary codicil in 1284. The panels form a harmonious triptych with 15 compartments containing 320 relics. At the foot are the keys which, according to tradition, Saint Ferdinand received on reconquering Seville in 1248.

Do not leave the the Sacristy without pausing to admire at close-hand one of the four gilded silver candlesticks, known as the «Gigantes», made by Hernando de Ballesteros the Younger between 1579 and 1581, and restored by Laureano del Rosal in 1705.

Chapel of El Mariscal: exhibition room.

Sacristy Mayor: Monstrance of Arfe. ▷

At the rear, on the right, is a tiny corridor leading to the Patio de los Oleos, which dates back to the 16th century, is sustained by two slender columns made of pink jasper and contains a souvenier shop.

On the other side is a door leading to the Patio del Cabildo, also known as the Patio del Mariscal, built in the 16th century. The design is by Asencio de Maeda, with carvings by Hernán Ruiz II, the master stone-masons being Manuel Fernández and Diego de Caravallo. The grillework is by Rodrigo de Segovia. In the centre is a fountain of red jasper. At the rear, in a display cabinet, are three 16th-century patriarchal crosses, outstanding of which is the sumptuous one made of white glass. The stones and glass were cut between 1527 and 1530 by the silversmith Diego de Vozmediano and the stonemason Juan Bautista. The «manzana» is by Hernando de Ballesteros the Elder, between 1552 and 1553.

Antecabildo and Chapterhouse: the courtyard gives access to the space known as the Antecabildo, a small crossing place and a fine example of the Mannerist style, designed by Hernán Ruiz in around 1560 and completed by Asencio de Maeda in 1583. It has a vault of splayed stone ending in a lantern, and its walls are finely decorated. It is separated from the Chapel of El Mariscal by a stone doorway, with lintel and jambs of jasper. (But we will go this way later).

On the right of the Antecabildo, a clean, narrow corridor leads us to the Chapterhouse, a solemn, majestic space which is, according to Alfonso Jiménez, present *maestro mayor* of the cathedral, «one of the most surprising examples of 16th-century

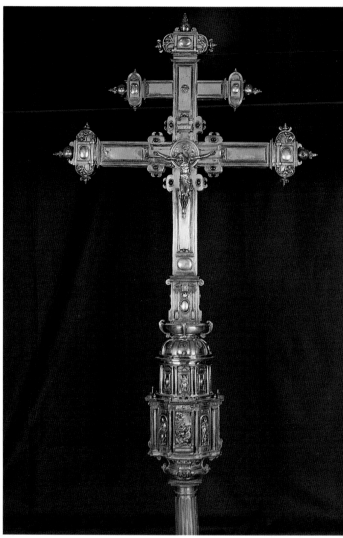

Reliquary bust of Sant Rosalia.

Patriarchal cross (Merino).

European architecture, due not only to its elliptical groundplan, pre-dating even similar Italian elements, but also to the existence of a suspended upper order articulating the walls. These leave the lower third of the walls bare, with all the plastic effects concentrated in the upper two-thirds» («La Catedral de Sevilla», Ed. Guadalquivir, 1984, p. 207).

Construction of the space was commenced by Hernán Ruiz in 1558 (after the Chapter rejected a Gothic-style project by Diego de Riaño), and was terminated by Asencio de Maeda in the last decade of the 16th century. The seats are in leather, the Archbishop's chair, a Renaissance piece, made in 1592 by Diego Velasco. The first third of the walls is covered by crimson cloth, crowned by a sumptuous Doric entablature. This is followed by another third, Ionic, featur-

ing marble reliefs springing out from the vault at the cornice, at the lower part of which are a combination of paintings and skylights, the paintings depicting the coat of arms of the Chapter (the Giralda and two bunches of lilies), a theme repeated in the vault. Among the reliefs, outstanding is that of the Assumption over the Archbishop's chair. In all, there are 16, designed by Canon Francisco Pacheco, uncle of the artist. Above the relief of the Assumption is the most splendid *Inmaculada*, by Bartolomé Esteban Murillo, painted for this site in 1668, the canvas following the curve of the vault. Also by Murillo are the portraits of Sevillian saints: King Ferdinand, Leandro, Rufina, Justa, Pío, Isidoro and Hermenegildo. The floor, of centrifugal lines, combines marbles and jaspers, rather worn now. The plan, according to Alfonso Giménez, is based on Michaelangelo's design for the Piazza del Capitolio in Rome, though the Sevillian work predates it (op. cit., p. 207). Few more monumental rooms could be found for the sessions of the Chapter. Leaving the Chapterhouse, to the right, is the last of the museum areas, a richly-coffered rectangular room (formerly the Sala de Ornamentos). It is presided over by a splendid statue of Joseph with the Child, carved by Pedro Roldán in 1664. In the centre is the so-called *Custodia Chica,* a smaller monstrance dating back to

the late-16th century, attributed to Francisco Alfaro and made for the Dominican Convent of Gibraleón. It was acquired by the Chapter in 1757, after which a reliquary was added to it to hold the Holy Bone, donated by Cardinal Rodrigo de Castro, who had received it from Empress Maria of Austria, sister of Philip II, with pontifical document of authenticity. It is carried in the procession which takes place at Corpus Christi. Next to it is the original model, in wood, for the Arfe monstrance.

Chapel of El Mariscal: panelled altarpiece.

Exhibition room: statue of Saint Joseph with Child, by Pedro Roldán.

Antecabildo.

Vault of the Chapterhouse. ▷

Contents of the display cabinets, starting at the right of the main entrance: gold and enamel monstrance with 1,336 precious stones, the work of Ignacio Thamaral, donated by Isabel Pérez Caro and first used during the Corpus Christi celebrations of 1729. Its viril (smaller monstrance kept in it) is that kept in the Custodia de Arfe. It was used by John Paul II on his second visit to Seville for the XLV International Eucharistic Congress. Another large monstrance, known as «El Grande», in gold, silver, emeralds, diamonds and 1,500 pearls adorned with bunches of grapes, was donated by Cardinal Solís in the second half of the 18th century. Next, the Urn of the Easter Thursday Monument, with a body of solid gold, engraved in Rome by Luis Valadier in 1781, and donated by Canon Jerónimo del Rosal, along with

two keys on gold chains. Two censers, both in gold, by Antonio Méndez, donated in 1791 by Manuel Paulín de la Barrera. Gold altar cruet with bell, made in México in the 18th century. 18th-century water jugs. This row of cabinets ends with the splendid altar cross and candelabrae of Cardinal Hurtado de Mendoza, made in Toledo between 1486 and 1502; *portapaz* with the Virgin in the centre (Paris School, dated between 1317 and 1322), which belonged to Philip V of France, bequeathed to the Cathedral from the belongings of Cardinal Palafox, along with another, Classical *portapaz*.

Left: reliquary bust of Saint Rosalía, made in Palermo in 1681 by Antonino Lorenzo Castelli and donated by Cardinal Palafox. Gold chalice and ciborium, incrusted with emeralds and rubies, dating back to the

Chapterhouse: Immaculate, by Murillo.

Chapterhouse: Relief of the Assumption.

18th century, used in the Easter Thursday ceremonies. Two 18th-century Mexican cups with their plates, in engraved gold, donated by Bizarrón, Archbishop de México, with glass beadwork salver. Pre-Gothic altar cross. *Lignum crucis,* known as that of Constantino, anonymous early-16th century work donated by Archbishop Alonso de Fonseca, reformed in 1562 by Ballesteros the Elder; reliquary of Saint Clement, in the form of a gold chalice, its cup formed by a large agate crowned by the figure of Saint Clement, in gold, donated by the bishop of Scalas in 1518; glass beadwork salver. Romanesque silver cross, one of the oldest pieces in the Cathedral, in agate and gilded bronze, dating back to the 13th century and restored in the 16th century. Three *portapaces,* outstanding of

which is that of Santa Ana with Virgin and Child, of absidal structure and in gilded silver, engraved with a mark leading it to be attributed to Martín de Oñate; Baroque salver. In the last cabinet are two more recent works: processional crowns of the Virgen de los Reyes and the Child, made in 1904 for the canonical coronation of El Niño (pontificated by Cardinal Spínola) by Manuel Ordóñez and Pedro Vives, the first paid for by popular subscription and the second donated by Gracia Fernández Palacios. They are made of gold and encrusted with 11,960 precious stones.

The *Chapel of El Mariscal,* reached through the main door of the room we have just visited, has a magnificent altarpiece of panels reminiscent of the style of

Chapterhouse. ▷

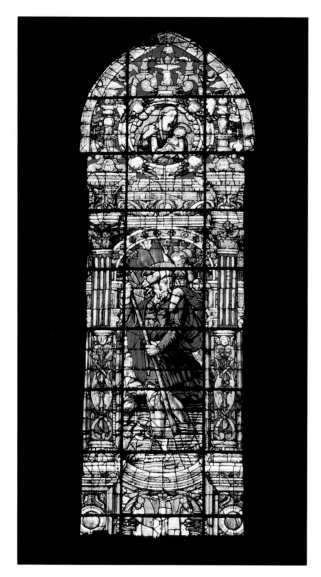

Puerta de la Campanilla: stained-glass windows of Saint Christopher.

Altar of Saints Justa and Rufina (Duque Cornejo). ▷

ings by Antón Ruiz, dated around 1544. This chapel is also known as that of «Saint Antonio Chico», due to the small figure of the saint adjoining the wall, of little artistic merit, but fervently worshipped popularly.

Over the Puerta de La Campanilla is a painting representing Saint Roque, by Antonio de Afián (16th century) and a sumptuous stained-glass window depicting Saint Christopher, made by Arnao de Flanders in 1546.

Following the east aisle of the Cathedral, we come to the Chapel of the Concepción Grande, thus known due to the large-than-life statue of the Virgin which presides over it, by the sculptor Alonso Martínez and completed in 1658. The altarpiece is Baroque and contains the first example of Solomonic column in Seville. At the top, Christ on the Cross, angels at his feet, archaic in style, but reformed when this altarpiece was installed, between 1656 and 1658. The front stained-glass window is by Arnao de Flanders (1550), but has been much restored. It represents the Martyrdom of Sain Peter. The side window is dated 1789, though it contains elements from a previous work. This chapel contains the rectorate office of the Cathedral.

The outer walls of the Capilla Mayor are adorned with series of terracotta sculptures on consoles and under baldachins, Gothic but with Renaissance tendencies, little-studied according to Professor Hernández Díaz. They are attributed to Miguel Florentín, Juan Marín and Diego de Pesquera and form a highly elegant, harmonious whole.

At the trasaltar, opposite the entrance to the Capilla Real, is an interesting polychrome terracotta sculpture attributed to Florentín: the Virgen del Reposo, popularly known as the Virgin of «Enhorabuena lo pariste» and to whose good offices pregnant women traditionally commend themselves. Below are two paintings by Sebastián de Llano Valdés, representing John the Baptist before the Sanhedrin and the Vocation of Saint Matthew, dated 1668, featuring excellent draughtsmanship in the figures. Also hanging here is a painting representing the army of Giddian, traditionally attributed to Titian, a fine work of the Napolitan school, dating back to the mid-17th century.

Raphael, by Pedro de Campaña and Antonio de Afián (16th century). This chapel was donated by Diego Caballero, Marshall of La Española, and is dedicated to the Purification de Mary. It has an excellent grille by Pedro Delgado (16th century), designed by Hernán Ruiz and crowned by the Funeral of Christ. Above, stained-glass window by Arnao de Flanders (1556), with the Wedding of Mary and Joseph.

Leaving the Chapel of El Mariscal, on the right (intradós of the Puerta de La Campanilla) is one of the finest representations of saints Justa and Rufina (as always, protecting the Giralda), by Duque Cornejo, carried in the Corpus procession. On the other side is the Chapel of Santa Bárbara, containing ten paint-

Capilla Real: Urn of Saint Ferdinand.

Capilla Real. ▷

The Capilla Real

We now enter another world of art and history. The Capilla Real was founded as the royal burial-place in the Mosque-Cathedral by Sancho IV at the end of the 13th century, the present fabric was completed by the Chapter with the permission of John II, in a slow process finally culminated thanks to the insistence of Emperor Charles V. Work began in 1552, directed by Martín de Gainza, after whom Hernán Ruiz and Pedro Díaz Palacios took over before the work was completed by Juan de Maeda in 1575, though the grille, donated by Charles III and made by the engineer Van Der Borcht, is later. This grille is crowned by a sculpture of Saint Ferdinand receiving the keys of Seville from the Moorish king Axataf, by Jerónimo Roldán. The grille was installed in 1771.

The quadrangular groundplan of the chapel gives it an air of grandeur. The structure is Plateresque, with eight decorated pilasters, large dome with coffers adorned with the heads of Spanish monarchs, and lantern. The apse represents an angelic glory. The chapel is highly-decorated with sculptures and has two stained-glass windows on the side walls, bearing the coat of arms of Spain and originally installed in 1574 by Vicente Menardo.

The religious work most highly treasured here is the statue of the «Virgen de los Reyes», thus-known as it came from the household of Ferdinand III. This is the most fervently-worshipped statue in Seville and sur-

Capilla Real: tomb of Alphonse X.

Capilla Real: tomb of Beatrice of Swabia.

rounding area, and leads an impressive procession every 15 August. It is said to have been a gift from Saint Louis of France to his cousin Saint Ferdinand and it is certainly true that the figure is reminiscent of that of the Regal Virgins of the circle of Chartres. The Virgin's face suggests the transition from Romanesque to Gothic (13th century), its fleeting, warm smile illuminating it. The Child is wholly Gothic, with ruffled hair and cheeky smile. The various elements combine harmoniously to form a splendid piece. Mary's hair is hidden by golden braids, and both figures are fitted with a mechanism, now in disuse, which allows the heads to be moved during the processions.

This statue, then, presided over the royal chapel of Ferdinand III. The people of Seville asked Ferdinand's son, Alphonse X, to donate it, and so he did, as is recorded in Cantiga CCCXXIV, donating it to the Iglesia Mayor (Cathedral) of the See. When the Capilla Real was completed, the Chapter installed the statue here, in an altarpiece by Luis Ortiz de Vargas between 1643 and 1649, and which also features the figures of Mary's parents, Joachim and Anne. It was crowned canonically by Cardinal Spínola y Maestre in 1904 and canonically declared Patron Saint of the Archidiocesis of Seville in 1946, during the pontificate of Cardinal Segura.

At the feet of the Virgin lies the mummified body of her faithful servant Ferdinand III, the Holy, in a florid silver urn made by Laureano de Pina between 1665 and 1719 and donated to the Chapter by Philip V. It is opened to reveal the holy king's body behind a glass

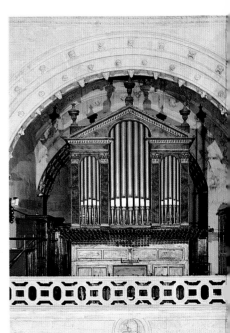

Capilla Real: Altarpiece of Saint Anthony.

Crypt: Virgen de las Batallas.

Capilla Real: organ, by Otín Calvete.

Capilla Real: Virgen de los Reyes (13th century).

Capilla Real: 18th-century font for holy water.

Coro in the Capilla Real.

panel every 30 May, his feast day, 23 November (anniversary of the conquest of Seville) and on the day marking the transfer of the remains to the new urn, on 14 May. The marble pedestal is inscribed with the glowing epitaph written by Alphonse X for his father, whom he worshipped:

"El más leal, el más verdadero, el más franco, el más esforzado, el más apuesto, el más granado, el más sofrido, el más homildoso, el que más temía a Dios and el que más le hacía servicio, el que quebrantó and destruyó a todos sus enemigos and el que alzó and honró a todos su amigos and conquistó the ciudad de Seville que es cabeza de toda España".

The memory of Saint Ferdinand took root in Seville, of which city he is patron saint. At the foot of the Chapel, mid-way up and adjoining the walls are the tombs of Alphonse X and his mother, Beatrice of Suabia, constructed in 1948 to commemorate the seventh centenary of the conquest of Seville, in stone and alabaster: the tomb of Alphonse X, by Antonio Cano and Carmen Jiménez; and that of Beatrice of Suabia, by Juan Luis Vasallo. Nearby are two beautiful fonts for holy water, dating back to the 18th century.

The crypt is entered on either side of the Urn of Saint Ferdinand and contains the resting-place of various monarchs, among them Peter I and his wife, Mary of

Crypt in the Capilla Real.

Sword of Saint Ferdinand.

Padilla. The central cabinet displays the *Virgen de las Batallas,* a Gothic figure worked in ivory (13th century), carried by Saint Ferdinand on his saddletree during battles.

Over the tribune to the left is the organ made by Otín Calvete in 1807. From here, we pass through to the Chapterhouse of the Capellanes Reales, in whose central cabinet is displayed the sword of Saint Ferdinand, carried in procession by the mayor of Seville during the celebrations held in the Cathedral on 23 November, anniversary of the conquest of Seville; the king's buckles and spurs are also exhibited. Other cabinets contain jewels and other adornments of the Virgen de los Reyes, chalices and salvers, as well as the paten used to celebrate the first mass in México. Outstanding paintings housed here include Saint Ferdinand, by Murillo and the Virgen de

Capilla Real: treasure. Painting of Saint Ferdinand (Murillo).

Chapel of San Pedro: altarpiece.

Chapel of San Pedro: tomb of Fray Diego de Deza.

los Reyes under Baldachin, by Bernabé de Ayala. In the gallery on the right is the mahogany Coro of the Capellanes Reales, donated by Carlos IV, the altarpiece of San Antonio, from the studio of Luis Ortiz de Vargas, and a crucifix said to have belonged to Hernán Cortés.

Chapel of San Pedro: our visit does not end with the Capilla Real, for in the adjoining Chapel of San Pedro awaits us a small museum dedicated to Zurbarán. The altarpiece was assembled by Diego López Bueno in around 1625. All the paintings contained in it, except the Father Eternal crowning it, are by that grand master, Francisco de Zurbarán. In the centre, Saint Peter in pontifical dress, depicted between the stories of the Vision of the Impure Animals and the Tears of the Apostle. Above, the splendid Immaculate, large and lovely, flanked by scenes depicting the «Quo Vadis» and the Liberation of Saint Peter. The crowning Father Eternal dates back to the 18th century and replaces the original.

The walls feature paintings alluding to the life of Saint Peter Nolasco, brought here from the Convent of La Merced. They bear the unmistakable mark of Zurbarán, though Enrique Valdivieso believes that the series was begun by him and finished by his pupils, Francisco Reyna and Juan de Zurbarán (Catálogo de las Pinturas de la Catedral de Sevilla, 1978, pp. 114-116).

The stained-glass window featuring Saint Peter, over the altarpiece, is dated 1779 but contains elements

Painting by Zurbarán. *Chapel of San Pedro: painting by Zurbarán.* *Painting by Zurbarán.*

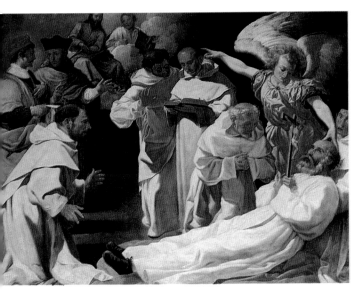

Altar of the Assumption.

by Arnao de Flandes; that on the wall, bearing papal attributes, is dated 1784 and was restored in 1929. The funeral monument is dedicated to Archbishop Fray Diego de Deza and features a Renaissance-style recumbent figure installed here in 1884, brought from the College of Santo Tomás, which was founded by Fray Diego himself.

Intradós of the Puerta de los Palos: the stained-glass window above is by Arnao de Vergara in 1535. A sumptuous work, the rising sun fills it with light. It represents Saint Sebastian, but is really a portrait of Emperor Charles V in period dress. Below is a painting of the same saint, by Antonio de Alfián (16th century).

On the right is the Altar of La Magdalena, nine recently-restored paintings, featuring that of the Apparition of Christ to Mary Magdalene *(Noli me tangere)* and an Assumption of the Virgin. Ceán Bermúdez attributes these works to Gonzalo Díaz (1449); but Enrique Valdivieso and others suggest that they are later (around 1537), with influences from Alejo Fernández, attributed to a pupil of his (Op. cit., p. 21).

On the other side of the door is the Altar of the Assumption, in relief, surrounded by excellent paintings, the work of Alonso Vázquez (1593). To one side is a door leading up to La Giralda.

Aisles of the north side

We now beginning the final section of our visit with contemplation of the aisles of the north side. Firstly, the Chapel of La Virgen del Pilar, whose origins in the Cathedral-Mosque are due to the Aragonese presence in the hosts of Saint Ferdinand on entering Seville. Grille dating back to 1717. Over it, a stained-glass window by Arnao de Flandes, with Entrance of Jesus into Jerusalem (1553). At the rear, the altarpiece featuring the fine terracotta figure of La Virgen del Pilar, by Pedro Millán (around 1500), considered the finest of that artist's works. The Virgin and the Child are in late-Gothic style. On either side, two figures representing saints Peter and Paul. On the Baroque lateral altarpiece was recently installed a statue of Saint Judas Tadeo, due to the enormous devotion this saint has acquired of late.

Now take the corridor from the Puerta del Lagarto to the Chapel of Los Evangelistas. Stained-glass window by Arnao de Flandes, Resurrection of Lazarus (1554). Inside the chapel, another by the same artist, depicting the Birth, also dated 1554. The altarpiece contains fine works by the Dutch painter Hernando de Esturmio, dated 1555: in the centre, The Mass of Saint Gregory and the Resurrection; on either side, the Four Evangelists; saints Justa and Rufina (showing the Giralda before the reforms carried out by Hernánd Ruiz) and saints Catherine and Barbera. In the opinion of Enrique Valdivieso, this is one of the most interesting pictoric sites in the Cathedral (Op. cit., p. 30). On the walls are eight Flemish paintings,

Chapel of the Virgen del Pilar: altarpiece.

Chapel of the Virgen del Pilar (Judas Tadeo).

Chapel of Los Evangelistas (16th century).

Chapel of Las Doncellas: altarpiece.

Chapel of Las Doncellas: grille.

among which outstanding is that of the Four Evangelists (17th century) and that of the Martyrdom of Saint Peter Arbués, a copy made in the early-19th century from an original by Murillo now in the Hermitage Museum. In the centre was recently installed part of the Corpus apparatus, previously in the Antecabildo. This change is not a success, as it cannot be seen well and obscures our view of the altarpiece.

Chapel of las Doncellas: one of the most beautiful grilles in the Cathedral, a Renaissance work completed in 1579. Over it is a stained-glass window featuring Mary Magdalene, by Arnao de Flandes (1554). In the interior, another by Arnao de Vergara (1534), with a two-fold theme: the Virgen of Misericord and the Annunciation. According to Villar Movellán, one of the most beautiful in the Cathedral, recalling

the compositions of Il Perugino and Raphael (La Catedral de Sevilla, 1977, p. 76).

The Baroque altarpiece is installed over a gallery adorned with tiles. The paintings were attributed to Cristóbal Morales by Professor Post Chandier due to their resemblance to a Burial of Christ in the Seville Museum of Fine Art. In the main body of the altarpiece: Saint Bartolomew, Saint Peter, Saint Thomas and Saint James the Younger. In the attic, Calvary, Saint Ambrose and Saint Augustin. On the bench, Saint Jerome, Saint Gregory and the presentation of the dowries to the damsels featuring the donor of the altarpiece, García de Gibraleón. Cristóbal Morales worked in Seville in the first half of the 16th century. The transept is reached through a small Renaissance grille.

Chapel of La Asunción: painting by Alonso Vázquez.

North wing of the transept

This is lighted by nine magnificent stained-glass windows. In the centre is a rose window by Arnao de Flandes and Arnao de Vergara in 1539, representing the Ascencion of the Lord. The others, beginning with that closest to the Coro are: Saint Leandro, Saint Lawrence, Saint Vincent and Saint Stephen (1548); Saint Cosme, Saint Damian, Saint George and Saint Hermenegild (1549); Saint Paul, Saint John the Baptist, Saint Roque (1551); The Coming of the Holy Spirit (1557), all by Arnao de Flandes, that of the Holy Spirit perhaps the last by Arnao de Flandes in this Cathedral; on the other side, the Resurrection, by Carlos de Brujas (1558); the next three by Arnao de Flandes: Saint Matthew, Saint Judas Tadeo, Saint Philip (1551); Saint Simon, Saint Bartolomew Saint James and Saint Thomas (1544); Saint John, Saint James, Saint Andrew and Saint Peter (1543).

Below the rose window is a large painting by Alfonso Grosso(1966), depicting the proclamation of the dogma of the Immaculate Conception: the face of the Virgin imitates that of the Macarena; that of the Archbishop, the factions of Cardinal Spínola y Maestre; whilst the Seises are also represented.

On the left inside the Puerta de La Concepción, leading to the Patio de los Naranjos, is the Chapel of the Asunción, with a painting attributed to the Italian artist Carlos Maratta by Céan Bermúdez, whilst Pérez Sánchez and others claim it to be by Gregorio Ferrari (d. 1726), of the Genoan school.

Much more interesting is the chapel on the right, with the outstanding *Virgen de Belén,* painted by Granada's famous son, Alonso Cano, between 1635 and 1637, with a certain Italianate inspiration, but with a personal touch as regards movement, colour and human warmth. Among the finest in this Cathedral, where there is so much artistic splendour. The grilles of the two chapels are also magnificent.

At the head is a large painting, a moving composition representing the Slaughter of the Innocents, attributed by Professor Evelina Borea to the Florentine artist Jacopo Fardella (Enrique Valdivieso, op. cit., p. 128). In any case, certainly a 17th-century Italian work.

Chapel of La Virgen de Belén (Alonso Cano - 1635).

Front of the Puerta de la Concepción: Slaughter of the Innocents.

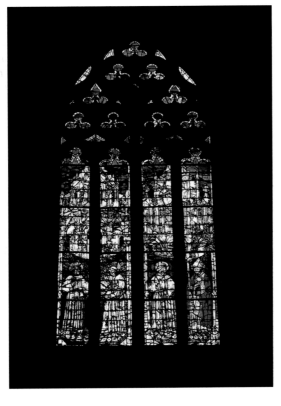

Chapel of San Francisco: stained-glass windows.

Altarpiece of Santa Teresa in the Chapel of San Francisco.

Chapel of San Francisco: Apotheosis of Saint Francis (Herrera the Younger).

Chapel of Saint Francis: over the grill, one of the oldest stained-glass windows in the Cathedral, by Enrique Alemán in 1478 and restored by Arnao de Flandes in 1538 (saints Anthony of Padua, Bernardino of Sienna, Francis of Assissi and Louis of Toulouse). Inside, another by Arnao de Flandes (1554-1556), one of the most beautiful, representing the stigmata of Saint Francis of Assissi.

The huge frame of the painting of Saint Francis is by Bernardo Simón de Pineda (1661). The Apotheosis of Saint Francis is a splendid painting by Francisco de Herrera el Mozo in 1657, a delight to the eye. At the top, the Imposition of the Chasuble on Saint Ildefonso, by Valdés Leal, dated 1661. The chapel also contains the small Altarpiece of Santa Teresa and a half-figure *Ecce Homo,* as well as some less interesting paint-

ings: Calle de La Amargura, Jesus with the Lamb, Presentation in the Temple, The Flight to Egypt and the fine Conversion of Saint Paul, attributed by Valdivieso to the Flemish painter Francken II (17th century).

Chapel of Santiago: the upper stained-glass window is by Enrique Alemán (1478) and features saints Justa and Rufina, James the Elder and Barbara. The interior, Renaissance in style, is by Vicente Menardo and features the Conversion of Saint Paul (1560).

The chapel contains many works of art. A huge Baroque frame by Simón de Pineda features an important painting by Juan de Roelas, representing Saint James at the Battle of Clavijo, an expressive composition with great movement dated 1609. At the top is a painting by Valdés Leal depicting the Martyr-

VERDADERA VIRTVD CON QDIMA IORRES PLANDOR A MIIIVS
TRE LINAGEM FLE VANTO A LA SILLA OBISPAL DE CALAHORRA Y DO
PVES A LA DE BVRGOS VLTIMA MENTE FV I ARCOBISPO DE SEVILLA BIV
INCVLPABLEMENTE Y NO CONTENTO CON PROCVRAR COMO BVEN PAS
TOR A VMENTAR LA GREI DEL SENOR QVE APACENTA VA FVNDEY DTE
AMPLISSIMAMENTE ESTE MONESTERIO PARA QVE EN EL HA I LA SENOR
HAS ALMAS CARRERA DE SALVACION Y MVCHOS POBRES PERMAN
CIENTE EL SOCORRO DEMI LIBERALIDAD PERDI LA VIDA EN TIEN
PO DE PESTE PORQ APLACAD OEL SENOR EN MI MITIGAS E SV IVST
YRA CON MIS OVEIAS Y DESPVES DEL ARGO DIA QVE ESTV VE SEP III
IADO EN LA YGLESIA METROPOLITANA DEMI CATHEDRA POR DII
GENCIA Y LAGRIMAS DEMIS ESPIRITVALES HIIOS FV I TRAIDO A ESTA
MI VGI ESI A DONDE CERCADO DE SVS PIAD OSOS TRABAIOS QVE SON
RVCTOS DE MI CHARIDAD Y ZELO ESPERANDO LA SEGVNDA ESTO
A REPOSO EN EL SENOR · DON GON CAL O DE MENA NATVRAL E GLED
VE IO AÑO I M · CCCC · I · FVE TRASLADADO · A ÑO · M · D · X C I III

Chapel of Santiago: tomb of Archbishop Gonzalo de Mena.

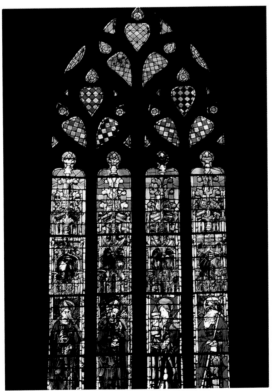

Chapel of Santiago: stained-glass windows.

Chapel of Santiago: 16th-century Pietà.

dom of Saint Lawrence (h. 1600). Over the altar table is a group representing the *Pietà* (Seville School, h. 1700).

Special mention deserves the tomb of Archbishop Gonzalo de Mena, founder of the Carthesian Monaster of Las Cuevas, who died in 1401. This is an early 15th-century Gothic tomb featuring a recumbent figure in alabaster. Also outstanding here is the glazed terracotta relief, in blue and white enamel, representing the *Virgen del Cojín,* by the Florentine artist Andrea de la Robbia (16th century), transferred to the Cathedral in 1885 and restored in 1909 by Joaquín Bilbao. Simply lovely.

The wall facing the main altarpiece displays a fine collection of paintings by Antón Pérez, mid-16th century Sevillian painter, brought here from the altarpiece in the Sacristía Mayor and dated 1547-48. They represent religious allegories and the Virtues. Originally, there were 14 paintings, but one was stolen recently.

What is more, after the «Magna Hispalensis» exhibition in 1992, four more paintings, by Simón de Vos, were installed here. These depict Biblical scenes. Also: a fine Saint Sebastian of Bayeux (18th century); and a Saint John by Francisco Polanco (17th century).

Opposite are the *Chapels of the Alabasters of the north side,* which match those of the south side near the Coro. In one is a Saint Gregory by Manuel García de Santiago (18th century). The most interesting feature is the Plateresque interior layout of the chapel and the grille, dated 1650. Next to it is the Chapel of the Virgen de la Estrella, whose Plateresque design cannot be appreciated, concealed as it is by the Baroque altarpiece (1695), the work of the carpenter Jerónimo Franco and the gilder José López. Fine figure of the Virgin (an illustrious devotee was the Countess of Barcelona during the years of her youth, spent in Seville), though it is difficult to identify the artist due to the restoration carried out in the 18th century. Villar Movellán speaks of its being attributed to Jerónimo Hernández and to the French artist Nicolás de León (La Catedral de Sevilla, 1977, p. 68). Let us now return to the two large chapels in the north aisle still to be visited.

Chapel of Santiago: relief of the Virgen del Cojín (Andrea de Robbia).

Chapel of Scalas: tomb of Bishop Baltasar del Río.

Chapel of Scalas: altarpiece. ▷

Chapel of Scalas: thus known due to the fact that it was donated by Baltasar del Río, Bishop of Scalas, Canon of Seville and table companion of popes Julio II and Leo X. Interesting Renaissance grille (1564), above which is a Gothic stained-glass window featuring the Apostles, by Enrique Alemán (h. 1478). The interior is modern, made in Munich by the House of Zettler in 1880, representing the Coming of the Holy Spirit, with two canons praying, harmonious and finely coloured.

The great Renaissance altarpiece, in marble and jasper, mounted over a gallery, contains the same motif in the centre. On the bench, the Miracle of the Loaves and Fishes and, at the top, the Father Eternal. The installation was completed on 5 May 1539 and it is attributed to the workshop of the Gazini of Bissone. It has recently been cleaned and is in splendid condition. Beneath is tomb made for the Bishop of Scalas, but it is empty, as the founder died in Rome in 1541 and was buried in the Church of Saint James in that city.

Facing the altar is another fine glazed terracotta figure by Andrea de la Robbia, the Virgen de la Granada, surrounded by Saint Francis of Assissi, Saint Domingo de Guzmán, Saint Casilda and Saint Sebastian. Interesting collection of paintings: *Pietà,* by Sebastián de Llanos Valdés (1666); Sagrada Familia, from the studio of Murillo; Adoration of the Shepherds, by Francisco Antolines (17th century); small panel with two scenes separated by a glued paper, representing the Kiss of Judas and *Ecce Homo* (anonymous imitator of Alejo Fernández), from the Chapel of los Dolores.

Chapel of San Antonio: Saint Anthony, by Murillo.

with its view of a classical patio. If you look closely, you will see a threadmark running around the figure of Anthony. This is because it was cut out and stolen one day in 1865. Such a famous work was not difficult for the police to trace, however, and it was recovered some months later in New York. Once returned to Seville, it was restored to its rightful place by Salvador Martínez Cubells, head restorer of the Prado Museum. Other paintings: Cándida Inmaculada, by Juan Roelas (1600); Virgin and Child, attributed to the «Mulato» Sebastián Gómez and in the style of Murillo; four works alluding to the Creation, (Flemish School, 17th century); and paintings of Saint Isidoro, Saint Leandro and saints Justa and Rufina, by an anonymous disciple of Zurbarán. Recently transferred to this chapel is a series of panels which were formerly installed at the entrance to the Sacristia Mayor. They

16th-century Renaissance baptismal font.

Chapel of Saint Antonio: the final point on our itinerary. Over the grille is a Gothic stained-glass window depicting the Four Evangelists, by Mateo Alemán (1478). The interior is Baroque and features the motif of saints Justa and Rufina and the Vision of Saint Anthony, by Juan Bautista de León in 1657, though dated 1685; in the last century, the blue background was changed to white in order to give it more light. The huge baptismal font is a good example of Renaissance art (16th century).

However, the most valued jewel in this chapel is the much-admired painting of the Vision of Saint Anthony, by Bartolomé Esteban Murillo (1656), with diagonal axis between the descending figure of the Child and the entranced Saint Anthony, with magnificent distribution of lights and spaces, down to the background

date back to the 16th century and feature a *Pieta* in the centre. Also recently transferred here is the painting Christ tied to the column with Saint Peter, of the school of Alonso Cano (17th century).

And so we come to the end of our visit. We leave you, and what better way, joined with the extasy of Murillo's Saint Anthony, contained in the splendid gilded polychromed frame made in 1667 by Bernardo Simón de Pineda.

And, if you so wish, please come with us now to admire the exterior of the Cathedral.

CATHEDRAL EXTERIOR

The structure of the historic centre of Seville, over which soars the magnificent figure of its Cathedral, impedes the building being seen from a distance from all angles. The best views are of the east-south angle, and the Cathedral can be admired from the Puerta del León of the nearby Alcázar, from the Door of the Diputación Provincial in the Plaza del Triunfo or from the Plaza de la Virgen de los Reyes, where the Giralda can be seen to best effect. At 9.30 in the morning, a small concert of bells can be heard here. Also recommended is the view from the interior of the Patio de Banderas of the Alcázar, at night, when both Cathedral and Giralda are illuminated as in a dream, in an unforgettably beautiful vision.

We begin our tour of the Cathedal exterior next to the Giralda, where we will pause at the end of our visit. As Seville Cathedral was constructed without an ambulatory, this is the only Gothic cathedral with doors in the sanctuary. The first of these, adjoining the Giralda, is the Puerta de Palos (thus-named due to those which gave access to the former Corral de los Olmos), in elegant late-Gothic style and decorated with terracotta figures of angels and prophets and a lovely tympanum featuring the Adoration of the Magi by Miguel Perrin in 1520. On the other side of the exterior of the Capilla Real (Renaissance, with large coats of arms) is the Puerta de La Campanilla (thus-named as

Portada del Príncipe.

it formerly contained a small bell used to call the Cathedral workmen), which matches the Puerta de los Palos and was also constructed by Miguel Perrin in 1522: its tympanum represents the Entry of Christ into Jerusalem.

As we tour the Cathedral perimeter, we can see the Renaissance dependencies of the Chapterhouse, the former *Contaduría Alta* and the *Sacristía Mayor*. The Puerta del Príncipe, whose name comes from the fact that it is opened for monarchs and heads of state on official visits from the nearby Reales Alcázares is to be found on the south side of the Cathedral, opposite the north side of the Archivo de Indias. Its central section is neo-Gothic, designed by the architect Adolfo Fernández Casanova between 1887 and

Portada de la Campanilla.

Portada de los Palos.

1895. The entrance is most elegant, beautifully illuminated at night and harmonising well with its early-Gothic surroundings; but it is unfinished, as is testified by the solitary saint on the right side of the arch. On the west side, the foot of the construction, we find: the Puerta del Nacimiento or Puerta of Saint Miguel, another jewel of the late-Gothic style, with impressive terracotta tympanum, the Birth of Our Lord, by Lorenzo Mercadante de Bretaña, also responsible for the terracotta sculptures of the four Evangelists, Saint Laureano and Saint Hermenegildo, all very naturalistic, reminiscent of the painting of Van Eyck. All these figures were completed between 1464 and 1467. The remaining sculptures in the archivolt are by Pedro Millán (1467). As occurs with this doorway's «twin», the Puerta del Bautismo, the canons and cathedral

technicians have been scratching their heads for years over what to do about the degradation these delicate sculptures are suffering due to the intense traffic on Avenida de la Constitución, but, despite all the studies and talks, nobody has yet come up with the solution.

Next is the huge Puerta de la Asunción, the main entrance, opened only to receive new archbishops and to bid them a last farewell in their funeral processions. Pope John Paul II also entered through this door on his visit to the Cathedral in 1982. Its present composition, neo-Gothic in style, was built up by stages over the length of the 19th century. The architectural work was directed by Ferdinand de Rosales between 1829 and 1833. The relief of the Assumption and the sculptures, many of which are

Apse of the Capilla Real, behind the Giralda.

missing, were completed by Ricardo Bellver in 1885. We meet Mercadante de Bretaña once more at the the Puerta del Baptisterio which, as its name suggests, provides entrance to the Baptistry, with tympanum depicting the Baptism of Jesus, but whose outstanding features are the terracotta figures: in the exterior, saints Justa and Rufina; in the interiors, Saint Leandro, Saint Isidoro, Saint Fulgencio and Saint Florentina (brother and sister saints of Seville all). The loveliest of the ancient entrances to the Cathedral.

Next, we come to the huge figure of the former Tabernacle, now the Parish Church, designed in the 17th century to have colossal proportions to match those of the Cathedral. In neo-Classical style, it was begun by Miguel de Zumárraga in 1618, continued by Ferdinand de Oviedo and completed by Lorenzo Fernández de Iglesias, being opened on the eighth day of Corpus in 1662. This church can be visited during religious ceremonies. It consists of a nave with transept, is very solemn and is presided over by an interesting altarpiece by Pedro Roldán.

Outside once more, turn right to reach the Puerta del Perdón, former access to the courtyard used for ritual ablutions when this was a mosque, now known as the Patio de los Naranjos (Courtyard of Oranges). The double horseshoe arch which was used as the main entrance to the mosque is preserved here, with its original Almohade doors, covered in bronze panels patterned with interlacing arches and Kufic inscriptions. The two huge chains are not the originals, which are kept in the Cathedral dependencies for greater security. The doorway was altered in 1520, when a relief depicting the expulsion of the merchants from the temple was added at the top and the terracotta statues of Saint Peter and Saint Paul, an angel and the Virgin of the Annunciation, all by Miguel Perrín, were added. These figures were recently restored. The interior of this doorway provides a lovely view of the Giralda.

Patio de los Naranjos. Reached from the interior of the Cathedral as part of the cultural itinerary. Two of the three original rows of pointed Moorish arches have been preserved. In the centre is a fountain with

Puerta del Sagrario.

Portada de la Asunción.

Puerta del Perdón.

Visigoth central bowl. The great entrance door to the Cathedral, the Puerta de La Concepción, was constructed in neo-Gothic style by the architect Fernández Casanova between 1895 and 1917.

Over the arches of the east side of the Patio is the huge Biblioteca Capitular (Chapter Library), which adjoins the Columbine Library, now rebuilt after it was demolished some years ago. The series of arches is known as the Nave del Lagarto (Nave of the Lizard), due to the lizard or croccodile which hangs from it, along with a huge elephant tusk, though these are wooden replicas of the originals which were, perhaps, like the other hanging objects, brought here as ex-voto offerings. The Puerta del Lagarto pertains to the original mosque, and has a small vault adorned with Moorish elements. Next to it is the Chapel of La Virgen de la Granada, with exterior of Mudéjar stuccowork and fine grille, completed in 1678. Inside are six columns with Visigoth capitals. The altarpiece and figures date back to 1721. The painting of Saint Onofre is the object of great popular devotion, and this is also often known as the Chapel of Saint Onofre. Nearby is an entrance to the Cathedral, with three Gothic figures in the tympanum: the Virgen del Reposo and kings David and Solomon.

Continuing our tour of the exterior of the Cathedral from the Puerta del Perdón, we pass by the dependencies of the Chapter and Columbine Library, with chapels adjoining the walls. Turning right, we can see the Moorish exterior of the Puerta del Largarto. And, finally, the Giralda.

The Giralda, Queen of Towers
(Entrance from inside the Cathedral)

The Giralda is, without a doubt, the Queen of all the towers in the world, for its slenderness, its elegance and its majestic combination of the Almohade art of the main section with the Christian belltower which now tops it.

It formed the minaret of the mosque, which began to be built in 1184 by Ahmed Ibn Baso and was completed in 1198 by Ali de Gomara. It was then crowned by four large golden apples, which could be seen from afar, gleaming in the sun. These fell in the earthquake of 1356, during the Christian period, and the tower was then completed by a simple belltower commissioned by King Pedro I. The drawings of it which have survived reveal a belltower of little elegance.

For this reason, the Chapter commissioned Hernán Ruiz to draw up a new project, the present belltower, one which harmonises Almohade with Renaissance art, and this element was built between 1558 and 1568. At the top is a lovely bronze statue of Faith, which revolves, acting as a weather vane, or

General view of the city featuring the Cathedral.

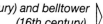

The Giralda has a Renaissance-style «crown» by Hernán Ruiz.

«Giraldillo», from whence the popular name of the entire tower.

The Almohade tower is entirely original and is formed of two parallel towers, one exterior and a smaller interior tower, its 35 ramps making it relatively easy to ascend (Isabel II once climbed it on muleback). Also notable is the fact that the thickness of the walls increases as we go higher. The exterior is made up of three vertical sections, the central part containing the window bays and balconies, the sides decorated with *sebka,* an ornate pattern carved in brick. The interior tower, higher than the outer tower, was enclosed as part of Hernán Ruiz's project.

The Christian section crowning the whole consists of four sections, one on top of the other, made of brick and stone with ceramic and ironwork ornamentation. The top section is the belfry, surrounding the upper part of the inner tower. There are 24 bells, now electrified, whose peals can be heard in the exterior. When the bells of The Giralda are rung «full-out», to mark the most solemn occasions, a veritable symphony in bronze peals out to fill the skies of Seville. This section is completed by four bronze lily urns, one at each corner. Next is the section containing the clock (installed in 1765 by the Franciscan Fray José Cordero), and of the Doric order. The 25th bell in the tower hangs here, from the clock itself. Above this is the "section of the stars" (called thus due to the decoration of stars on its frontons), of the Ionic order, narrower than the previous section and now circular rather than quadrangular, stylising the whole further. Next is the "section of the cannons", its name coming from the balls of the previous section, from which it springs. This section is also circular, but its diameter decreases from bottom to top, giving the impression of greater slenderness. Over it is a dome, *La Tinaja,* which supports the Giraldillo.

Studies were recently carried out to investigate the foundations and true height of the tower. It is simply sunk into the earth, it seems, its foundations going down to a depth of twenty metres, after which springs a powerful stone socle, on whose eastern side is a small niche for the Virgen de los Olmos, a Gothic figure which has now been replaced by a replica. Until recently, Aníbal González's claim that the height of

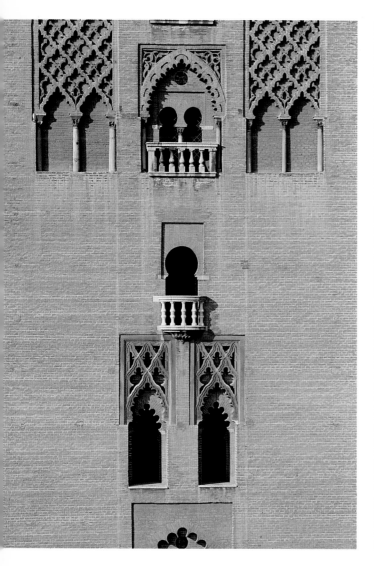

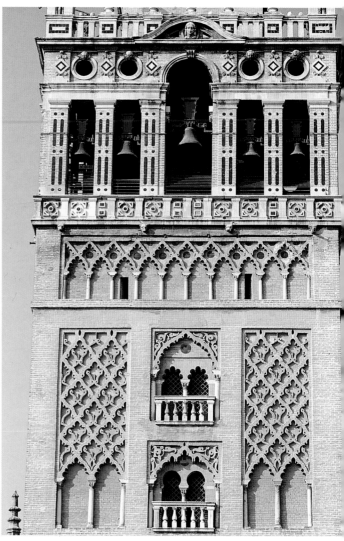

Almohade features of the Giralda tower.

Bell-tower.

the tower was 93.90 metres was taken to be true, but the architect José Mayor Cabeza, who worked on the recent restoration of the Giralda gives an exact height for it of 101.29 metres. According to Alfonso Jiménez, the Cathedral's present Master of the Fabric, from the base at street level to the very top, the Giralda weighs 19,045,975 kilos: to carry it on an imaginary train, this would require 1,900 wagons and be pulled by 74 engines, with a length of 13 kilometres 786 metres (Amalio García del Moral, The Giralda, Sevilla, 1987, p. 257).

We can understand, then, that the Giralda in Seville is indeed the queen of towers, making even its sisters, the Hassan Tower in Rabat and the lovely Kutubiya in Marakech, look small.

You may leave the unique city of Seville and, from your car, the train, the airplane, you will see the top of the Giraldillo like the elegant *peineta*, or comb, of a slender woman, bidding you farewell. The Giralda stands out, a splendid landmark, and the people of Seville wake every day to see it renewed and alive, in all its wealth and solidity. In it, Hernán Ruiz fully complied with the instructions given to him by the Sevillian canons when they told him to inscribe on the clock stage of the Giralda the motto from the Book of Proverbs «Turris fortissima nomen Domini» - «the name of the Lord as a strong tower». The Giralda is our welcome and our farewell.

Spectacular view of the Giralda, illuminated at night. ▷

CONTENTS